The Ex-Isle Of Erin

THE EX-ISLE of ERIN

FINTAN O'TOOLE

NEW
ISLAND
BOOKS

The Ex-Isle of Ireland
was first published in March 1997
in Ireland by
New Island Books,
2 Brookside,
Dundrum Road,
Dublin 14,
Ireland.

Copyright © Fintan O'Toole, 1996

ISBN 1 874597 49 9

Grant-aided by the
Arts Council

New Island Books receives financial assistance from
The Arts Council (An Chomhairle Ealaíon),
Dublin, Ireland.

Cover design by Jon Berkeley
Cover photo "Famine eviction scene, Model World,
Newtownmountkennedy, Ireland"
by Anthony Haughey
Typeset by Graphic Resources
Printed in Ireland by Colour Books, Ltd.

Exile, *n.* One who serves his country by residing abroad, yet is not an ambassador.

An English sea-captain, being asked if he had read "The Exile of Erin", replied: "No, sir, but I should like to anchor on it." Years afterwards, when he had been hanged as a pirate after a career of unparalled atrocities, the following memorandum was found in the ship's log that he had kept at the time of his reply:

Aug. 3rd 1842. Made a joke on the ex-Isle of Erin.

Coldly received. War with the whole world!

- Ambrose Bierce, The Devil's Dictionary

Acknowledgements

Journalists, like Pavlov's dogs, respond to stimuli, usually the terror of the deadline. Most of the pieces collected here were written in response either to commissions from the *Irish Times,* or to invitations from other publications and institutions. I am enormously grateful to Conor Brady, editor of the *Irish Times* for the freedom to pursue sometimes contrary ideas, and to Patsey Murphy, Sean Flynn, Paddy Woodworth, and Peter Murtagh who indulge them on their pages.

A slightly shorter version of *News from Nowhere* was published in *Granta* (number 53, spring 1996), and commissioned by Ian Jack, whose influence and encouragement were invaluable.

An Island Lightly Moored began life as a response to Anthony Haughey's brilliant exhibition of photographs at the Gallery of Photography in Dublin, *The Edge of Europe,* and I am grateful to him both for that and for permission to use one of the photographs from that exhibition on the cover of this book.

I Gotta Gal in Kalamazoo results from an invitation to talk to a conference on de Valera's Ireland issued by Professor Dermot Keogh at University College Cork. The essay *Setting Foot on Arch Hill* was written for a book edited by Jim McLaughlin of UCC. The Oscar Wilde essay was written for a projected book on Wilde being edited by Jerusha McCormack of UCD. The essay on Francis Stuart was written for a special issue of *Writing Ulster* (number 4, 1996) devoted to his work and edited by Bill Lazenbatt. The essay on Paul Durcan was written for the New Island book, *The Kilfenora Teaboy*, edited by Colm Toibin in 1996.

Parts of an address to an Ireland Association conference in Bangor, County Down, figure in the introduction. Parts of an essay for the *Labour in Art* exhibition at the Irish Museum of Modern Art in 1994 and of an essay written for

Desirs d'Irlande, edited by Catherine de Saint Phalle and Paul Brennan, have also been cannibalised.

I would like, too, to acknowledge the pervasive influence of the superb historical essays in *The New York Irish*, edited by Ronald Bayor and Timothy J. Meagher (published in 1996 by the Johns Hopkins University Press), and to thank Walter J. Walsh for bringing them to my attention.

Finally, my thanks to Dermot Bolger, who commissioned this book and to Frances O'Rourke, who edited it, for forgetting to panic. And my love and thanks, as ever, to Clare Connell.

To Samuel and Fionn,
with love

Contents

The Way We Are

INTRODUCTION

Yesterday the Empire, Tomorrow The World

In 1996, arguably for the first time in recorded Irish history, it became possible to understand the Republic of Ireland without reference to Britain. It was no longer possible to blame British colonialism, the nightmare of a benighted past, for the country's problems. It was no longer possible to envisage Irishness as merely the other side of Britishness. Seventy five years after the signing on December 6th 1921 of the Anglo-Irish Treaty establishing the Irish Free State, Ireland lost one of the key ingredients of its political and cultural make-up. After centuries of imagining itself in the shadow of a bigger, more powerful, and above all richer neighbour, it was faced with the necessity, not just to think again, but to find a whole new way of thinking. In terms of mental geography, Ireland ceased to be an island off Britain. After centuries of sending its people into exile, it became itself an ex-isle.

At one level, 1996 could be described as the apotheosis of the Free State, the year that Irish independence lost its temporary, unfinished, provisional character and took on a permanent look. Towards the end of the year a number of odd, stray occurrences began to cohere into a pattern. One was the 75th anniversary of the Anglo-Irish Treaty under which the State was established, and the fact that, at the age of 75, it is hard to go on pretending that you are not really responsible for what you have become.

Another was a successful Dublin summit of the European Union, in which Britain was so obviously an inconsequential and edgy presence on the margins while Ireland, holding the presidency, was at the centre of things, comfortable and competent. For centuries, England was phlegmatic, assertive, and businesslike, while Ireland was unsettled, uncertain, fretful about its national identity and place in the world. Now, the roles had been reversed: it was in England (and also, of course, in Scotland and Wales) that questions like nationality, sovereignty and identity were sites of confusion and contest, while the Republic of Ireland seemed, in 1996, to have gone beyond all that.

A third symptom was the fact that the Free State itself, so long regarded as a dour and grudging surrender of romantic destiny to contingent pragmatism, acquired, through Neil Jordan's film *Michael Collins*, its own astonishing glamour, its own myth of origin in which the stolid burghers of Cumann na nGaedhael suddenly became Hollywood stars, sexy and heroic.

But most of all there was the sensational, if largely unreported, fact that, in 1996, the Republic of Ireland produced more wealth per head of population than the United Kingdom. As recently as the early 1970s, after the last great boom time for the Irish economy, gross domestic product (GDP) per head of population in the Republic was half that of the UK. In 1995, if the EU average for GDP per head was 100, Ireland's was 95.1 and the UK's 98.3. But right at the end of 1996, Eurostat and the European Commission estimated that for 1996 the figures were 100.7 for Ireland and 98.9 for the UK. And they expected this gap to widen, so that by 1998 it will be 106.3 for Ireland and 99.6 for the UK.

And this shift, of course, coincided with preparations for the symbolic end of the British Empire itself. At the end of 1996, Simon Winchester pointed out in *Granta* that in September 1944, British imperial possessions contained a total population of 760,774,473 people. As of July 1st 1997, with Hong Kong's reversion to China, the figure is 168,075 people.

But more was ending than just an anchronistic Empire. The idea of Britain itself, by which Ireland had calibrated its own self-understanding, was bound up in that lost Empire. As the British political theorist David Marquand has put it 'Imperial Britain *was* Britain. The iconography, the myths, the rituals in which Britishness was embodied were, of necessity, imperial, oceanic, extra-European: they could not be anything else. Empire was not an optional extra for the British; it was their reason for being British, as opposed to English, or Scots, or Welsh. Deprived of Empire and plunged into Europe, 'Britain' has no meaning.'

What was most striking, however, was not just that Ireland was moving away from Britain, but the paradox that alongside that process was one in which the differences between Britishness and Irishness were narrowing to almost nothing.

If you look back now on the writings of Michael Collins, Eamon de Valera, or any of the political or cultural leaders of Irish nationalism, what is striking is the way in which they all accept implicitly that there is such a thing as a 'British civilisation', a way of life that is not confined to the island of Britain but that is, through the Empire, a presence in every continent, a structure of thought and feeling that people all over the world have to accept or reject. What defined Ireland was the fact that it had opted for rejection. Samuel Beckett's jokey reply to the question "Vous etes Anglais, Monsieur Beckett? "("You are English, Mr Beckett?") — *"Au contraire."* — could have been embroidered on the national flag. Being Irish was the opposite of being British.

When the Irish Free State was first established, and for many decades thereafter, talk of Irishness and Britishness as different, and opposed, world views may have been a gross oversimplification, but it made some sense. Irish identity *was* primarily rural, British primarily urban. Irish identity *was* primarily Catholic, British primarily Protestant. The Irish economy *was* primarily agricultural, the British primarily industrial. Irish nationalism *was* inward-looking and imbued with the values of self-sufficiency, British nationalism outward-looking and imperial.

As they had been constructed historically, the conflicting identities of British Protestantism and Irish Catholicism were statements not just about religious belief or political allegiance or even about the intertwining of the two. They were also — crucially — statements about much more mundane aspects of peoples's lives. They said, or were supposed to say, a great deal not just about how you voted or where you went to church, but about where you lived, how many children you had, what kind of work you did. Those contradictions operated, of course, not just *between* Ireland and Britain, but *within* Ireland itself— mostly, but by no means exclusively, between North and South. And this is why the conflict in Northern Ireland has had such a terrible hold — it has seemed to operate at the most intimate level as well as at the most abstract.

It is not just that the North was largely Protestant and largely industrial, while the South was largely Catholic and largely agricultural. It was that both North and South saw their respective religious identities as being bound up with their economic state. As it was presented ideologically, the North was industrial *because* it was Protestant. The South was agricultural *because* it was Catholic.

On the one side, the industrial might of Belfast — the shipyards, the engineering works, the linen mills — expressed a specifically Protestant spirit of endeavour and enterprise. This notion was given intellectual respectability by social theorists like Max Weber, and a less respectable reinforcement by the actual exclusion of

Catholics from much industrial employment, making for a self-fulfilling prophecy of the nastiest kind.

On the other side, Catholicism in Ireland had long been a nationality as much as a religion. The words "Irish Catholic" did not denote merely a person of a specific faith born in a specific country. They had also come to stand for some third thing born out of the fusion of the other two — a country, a culture, a politics. Catholicism in Ireland has been a matter of public identity more than of private faith. For most of its history, the Republic of Ireland was essentially a Catholic State, one in which the limits of law and of behaviour were set by Church orthodoxy and the beliefs of the Catholic bishops.

The Republic's relative economic underdevelopment was a necessity which became a kind of Catholic virtue in the official rhetoric of the State. Daniel Corkery's famous definition of Irishness as characterised by Land, Nationality and Catholicism remained ideologically potent well into the 1970s. The idea that authentic Irishness was both rural and Catholic was perhaps a way of making the best of a bad job, but it implicitly conceded the idea that urban and industrial culture was better suited to Protestantism than to Catholicism.

At the level of everyday life "Britishness" and "Irishness" were not just political concepts, but real expressions of a great deal that was fundamental to existence: whether you lived in a city or a village, what kind of job you did, whether or not you used contraception, how you thought about foreign countries. These distinctions were always crude but they were also effective. You could actually tell an awful lot about peoples' mundane realities — their jobs, their houses, the number of children they were likely to have, even their sex lives — once you had slotted them into the categories of "Irish" or "British".

Almost none of this is true anymore. Rural Ireland, the pastoral landscape that used to be contrasted to the North's primarily urban and industrial image, has disappeared. In *Poverty in Rural Ireland* (edited by Chris Curtin, Trutz Haase and Hilary Tovey), published in 1996, the sociologists John A. Jackson and Trutz Haase question whether it makes sense any more to talk about rural and urban Ireland as distinct societies. They point to growing numbers of people who live in the countryside and commute to the cities for work, the fact that inner cities are experiencing the kind of depopulation that used to be regarded as a rural phenomenon, the significant decline in the number of people living in the countryside who are actually engaged in agriculture, and the location of multinational industries in "rural" areas. "Factors such as media access, especially television, travel, tourism, and the growing diversification of consumer products have contributed to the incorporation of the rural population into the global economy and society." As a result, "the populations of rural and urban areas are coming increasingly to resemble each other".

In 1991, for the first time ever, fertility in the Republic fell to a level where births are just replacing deaths. This in itself was evidence of a massive change in the relationship between men and women, and in the relationship of ordinary Irish people to their Church. It meant that Irish Catholics were now using artificial contraception as a standard practice, even though the Catholic church continues to regard it as a sin.

Since then, the political power of the Catholic Church in the Republic has been utterly undermined by the long-term process of secularisation and the short-term one of scandal. For the Catholic Church, the final passage of divorce legislation in 1996 symbolised a much greater loss of authority. Catholics have become markedly Protestant in their attitudes to Church teaching, exercising the same rights of individual conscience as their Protestant neighbours do.

Just as, throughout Europe, the industrial revolution and Protestantism tended to advance hand-in-hand, the new prosperity created by Ireland's post-industrial revolution also saw an ambivalent kind of mass conversion to Protestantism. An MRBI poll for the *Irish Times* in December 1996 indicated that the most important tenet of Protestantism — the right of individual conscience — is now accepted by the great majority of Irish Catholics. Just a fifth of Catholics said that they followed the teaching of their church when making "serious moral decisions", compared to 78 per cent who said they would follow their own conscience.

At the beginning of 1995, after the worst year in the modern history of the Irish Catholic Church, the State archives opened to the public some documents from a previous, more triumphant, period. State papers revealed that in 1948, the Church and the then Government had seriously discussed the idea, put forward by the Archbishop of Tuam, of banning young women from leaving Ireland at all, so as to protect them from "moral, national and social perils". The proposal was eventually rejected as impractical, but the sympathetic hearing it received reminded Irish people, at the Church's lowest point, of just how powerful it had been.

What made the release of these papers all the more poignant was that it coincided with a story that turned their logic on its head, and that suggested that at least some of the "moral, national and social perils" that Irish innocents needed to be protected from were within the Church itself. In June 1994, a Catholic priest, Fr Brendan Smyth, was convicted in Northern Ireland of sexual offences against four children. This was in itself a serious matter for the Church, but it was by no means the first such conviction of a Catholic priest or brother. What caused perhaps permanent damage to the Church was an investigation by Ulster Television which showed that Fr Smyth had been known within the Church to be a dangerous paedophile since at least the early 1960s. It is grimly ironic, but entirely appropriate, that the Smyth scandal was the story of a transient man, a man whose life did not recognise borders that no longer mean much. The fact that he committed his crimes in Northern Ireland, in the Republic, in Britain, in America, was a vivid and unsettling reminder to Irish people that they were living in a world that is no longer containable within simple expressions of national or ethnic identity.

People in Ireland and Britain now watch the same television programmes, work in the same kinds of jobs or face the same despair of unemployment, and live with the same pressures in their personal and family lives. You can no longer use the terms "British" and "Irish" as cyphers for a range of unspoken attitudes and activities. In effect, Britishness and Irishness have become political identities *only*.

The extra load of meaning with which the words "British" and "Irish" were burdened should therefore have been lifted long before the 1990s. As the Republic became urbanised, secularised and industrialised, its people were leading the kinds of lives that had once been identified with Britishness. And equally profound changes had taken place in Protestant British identity. The certainties of Protestant existence have crumbled along with the industrial revolution that created and sustained them. The symbols of Protestant pride — industrial skills, the Royal Family, the Empire — have ceased to guarantee anything but confusion. The Irish and British economies began to look more and more similar. But, in the context of the Northern Ireland conflict, where people were killing and being killed over notions of what it meant to be Irish or British, it was hard to see this.

The fact is that both unionists and nationalists had a vested interest in the image of the Free State as a decrepit, underdeveloped, impoverished backwater. For nationalists, that image supplied the necessary sense of grievance — look what the Brits have done to us, and if only we were free we would be the happiest, most prosperous people on

God's earth. For unionists it provided the necessary warning — look what we would be like if the boggy mediocrity of the South was allowed to seep across the border.

For nationalists, Ireland being a Third World country was a source of pride, lending the glamour of international anti-imperialism to a squalid ethnic conflict in an obscure corner of the First World. For unionists, the Republic being a Third World country allowed the rather comic illusion that Northern Ireland itself is a beleaguered outpost of threatened modernity. But either as an excuse for failure or a dire warning to stick to nurse for fear of something worse, the rich Republic of the mid-1990s, rolling in dollars and ecus, is of little use to either nationalists or unionists.

It is true, of course, that substantial amounts of the wealth produced in Ireland are drained off by the repatriation of profits by multinational companies and by the servicing of the still-formidable national debt. But however much was drained away, it didn't take an economist to see that an awful lot was left. What *Newsweek* magazine described in December 1996 as the "Emerald Tiger" ("No need to search the Far East. The best answers to Europe's economic problems are much closer to home. Ireland is booming.") was not so much on the prowl as on the razzle-dazzle. Economic growth of 6 per cent in 1996, on top of an 8 per cent growth rate in 1995, sent money pumping through the system.

The average price paid for a second-hand house in the Republic in 1996 was £71,592 — a full £10,000 higher than in 1995. In 1996, a dozen houses in Dublin sold for more than £1 million each. Each of the two major banking groups is estimated to have made profits in the region of £375 million in 1996. In Dublin's Financial Services Centre alone, there were around 250 executives earning over £250,000 a year each. Just three golf clubs — Druid's Glen, Mount Juliet and the K-Club — between them took in over £2.5 million in green fees during the year. About 115,000 new cars were registered in the Republic in 1996. About 400,000 holidays were booked with Irish travel agents.

In 1990, the Republic's consumers spent £16.3 billion on goods and services. In 1995, the figure was £22 billion. Even taking inflation into account, it is likely that in 1996 the Republic's consumers spent in real terms over £4 billion more than they did in 1990. For those who could afford the entrance fee, Ireland had entered the world's fair of global consumerism.

And yet, all this conspicuous consumption did not lead to a society at ease with itself. Normally, those who preside over such good times could expect to bask in the glow of national gratitude. Instead, the opposite has been the case. As wealth grew, so did an extraordinary popular scepticism about leaders of all sorts, to such an extent that the whole idea of authority — political, moral, religious — became utterly problematic.

The authority of the State itself had been eroded, at least partly because the public no longer seemed to associate good times with national politics at all. Ministers got to spend the billions of ecus flowing in from the EU's regional and social funds, but the public knew that it had people outside the State — mostly German taxpayers — to thank for them. Ministers got to announce huge industrial investments like IBM's 3,000-job project for Dublin or Intel's $1.5 billion investment in Leixlip, but the public knew that the real decisions had been taken on the far side of the Atlantic.

This is the paradox of the Republic in the aftermath of the British Empire: its national independence is underwritten by transnational corporations and by a supra-national European Union. Its sovereignty is a power that can be exercised mostly by giving it up. Its separation 75 years ago from one political and economic union, the United Kingdom, is justified by its membership of a bigger political and economic union, the EU. Its cultural distinctiveness lies not in any fixed inherited tradition but in the particular way that it reacts to an overload of global stimuli, taking possession of Anglo-American norms, putting its own stamp on them and exporting them back to England, America and the rest of the world.

One of the consequences of the disappearance of the British Empire as the unfailing source, if not of all the Republic's ills, then certaintly of all its excuses, is that there is no room anymore to define Irishness by what it is not. Beckett's *au contraire* has to be taken down from the mast.

The essays in this book are an attempt, partly to describe, partly to imagine, what might take its place. Whatever that will be, its context will be the globalisation of the world economy. That process is one in which instant communications have made it possible for transnational corporations to monitor developments in many parts of the world, to move goods, services, and even manufacturing plants rapidly, and to treat the world as a single marketplace. And although driven by economic and technological forces, it is above all a cultural process. Central to it is the idea that for the same products to be sold with the same advertising campaigns in every country, the values, desires and dreams of people everywhere must be assimilated to international norms.

The purpose of these essays is to suggest three things about globalisation. One is that that process is having a profound effect on Irish culture. A second is that justified complaints about "American cultural imperialism" can sometimes miss the point that American mass culture may well contain buried elements of other cultures. This is especially so in the case of Ireland, and it is one of the reasons why multinational pop culture can be used creatively, rather than merely consumed, by Irish people. The third is that globalisation is not a one-way process. It affects different cultures in different ways, and each culture also makes its own contribution to the shape of global forces. Because it has been in a real sense a global society long before the term "globalisation" was ever heard, this is especially true of Ireland. It has buried memories, forgotten histories, that offer it some useful precedents for engaging with, rather than being swamped by, the new realities. By remembering and re-imagining them, it can, perhaps, learn how to surf the global waves without drowning in a flood tide of blandness and amnesia.

GLOBAL IRISHMEN

Tony O'Reilly and the News From Nowhere

On the morning in December 1995 that Tony O'Reilly spoke at a conference in Belfast, his own newspaper *The Irish Independent* ran two full pages about the event. One of them was dominated by a stark black-and-white ad. At its centre was a map of Ireland. Around the map was the distinctive triple-bordered shape of a label familiar to devotees of tomato ketchup and baked beans. Within the borders, like five huge white islands looming over the northern coastline of the country, were the letters HEINZ. There was nothing else — no slogan, no exhortation, just this strange map of a small island in the Atlantic. Inside the jagged contours of its coastline, this country had no border, no features, no landmarks of history, none of the resonant names or contested zones of a place emerging from a dark and tangled past. It was a clear, uncomplicated space, a brand-image, a label that could be stuck on a billion sauce bottles.

And as he himself rose to speak that morning in the Europa Hotel, against a backdrop of cobalt blue emblazoned with the logo of Independent Newspapers and an abstract painting of the globe, Tony O'Reilly seemed the perfect citizen of an Ireland that had escaped from itself. He had been introduced as a man who, as the Irish head of a multinational company, H.J. Heinz, with expected sales this year of $9 billion, "encapsulates perfectly" the theme of the conference — global economics. And that image had been driven home by his own newspapers over many years. His *Sunday Independent* once devoted an eight-page colour supplement to him, with the heading "A Man For All Continents" and no fewer than 17 photographs of the proprietor: Tony O'Reilly with Henry Kissinger, Tony O'Reilly with Margaret Thatcher, Tony O'Reilly with Valery Giscard D'Estaing, Tony O'Reilly with Robert Mugabe, Tony O'Reilly stepping off his corporate jet, Tony O'Reilly with his beautiful first wife and six beautiful children.

As he began to speak, he laid out the colour supplement of his own personality for the admiring gaze of his audience. He is every inch the 60-year old smiling public man, at ease before an audience, in the way that only someone who has been a star since he was barely out of school can be. A rugby international at the age of 18, he still has the height and bearing of a sportsman, even if the smooth beauty of his youth has now become rugged, its effect more imposing than dazzling. Because he seems to take his own air of authority for granted, he can afford to be charming, even gossipy, knowing that the sense of intimacy he creates will not be taken advantage of.

He is a man for whom there is no clear distinction between the private and the public self, a man whose acquaintances all remark on the fact that almost every meal in one of his houses in Pittsburgh or in Ireland seems to be a public event, shared with friends, contacts, associates, people who are, for one reason or another, being wooed. One former business associate has described dinner at O'Reilly's Irish estate, Castlemartin, as "like spending an evening with Elvis and his bloody circus". One of those who has been wooed as part of an O'Reilly business venture remembers the brilliant mixture of private charm and public purpose: "I found him big, expansive, talkative. He tells funny stories, he's charming, he makes you feel that his wealth, his big house and his ambience are yours to enjoy, and that you're being given privileged and undivided access to that, and he uses all of that with very considerable skill. You need that kind of charm and loquaciousness and those gifts in business and in public life, and he's got them in abundance. You find yourself with a sense of intimacy with him in your conversation, because he's indiscreet, and he speaks about people he knows in a mischievous way, so you feel quite close to him. And then you hear that if any of his staff fail to call him 'Doctor O'Reilly', he hangs them up by their heels and pours boiling pitch down the front of their trousers."

The contradiction is present even in his name. He is universally known as Tony, except in his own newpapers, where he is always referred to as 'Dr. A.J.F. O'Reilly', the doctorate being a PhD in food marketing awarded by the University of Bradford in 1980 for a thesis he submitted on the launch of Kerrygold butter, his first great business coup. Yet in reality Tony and Dr A.J.F. are indistinguishable in the persona of a man on intimate terms with the whole world.

Even before his formal audience in Belfast, he presented that same package of public and private. He marked the stages of his own career — the rugby, the days in the 1960s as chief executive of a series of Irish state-owned food companies, his ascent into the highest echeleons of corporate governance at Heinz in the 1970s, his late development as a global media magnate — with anecdotes. And all the time, his own story was made to seem a parable of globalisation, of a man rising from a specific time and place into a great network of worldwide power. Even his jokes were global, flow charts parodying management styles in China, Britain, Italy, Saudi Arabia, Latin America, Ireland, and the United States, appearing on the screen beside him as he performed his accomplished warm-up act.

As he strode around the world in his ten-league boots, the petty details of Irish history, so recently strewn in the shape of twisted metal and torn flesh on the streets outside the hotel, dissolved into insignificance. Facing an audience of besuited businessmen, drawn from both sides of the

Irish border and both sides of the Protestant-Catholic divide, he felt confident enough to tease them with a small political joke. His lecture, he announced, would be called "The island of Ireland — United". He paused just long enough to hear the strain in the room, the jerk of raw nerves being touched by the cruel point of politics. And then, his craggy face broken by a small smile, he picked up his sentence: "... to a global economic system."

After the jokes, he started to talk about history. He explained to his audience, with the help of slides, and as if they didn't know this, that we are at the end of the 20th century. The century, he said, is a triptych. In the first panel are two brutal world wars. In the second is a 45-year period of geo-political equilibrium and dramatic economic growth. And in the third, "here we are", in a new age of "capital ruthlessly seeking the best rate of return", of "the emergence of the global consumer". The 20th century, he said, was dominated by ideological competition, but the 21st will belong to commercial competition.

The slide now is made up of a large picture of O'Reilly's friend Nelson Mandela and a smaller one of Yitzhak Rabin and Yasser Arafat shaking hands, with the caption "The Collapse of Communism and the Promise of Peace". It looks like the end of history, and he mentions that Francis Fukayama wrote a book of that name after the demolition of the Berlin Wall.

For Tony O'Reilly, the great symbolic event of the last decade was not so much the fall of the wall as the opening of the first McDonald's in Moscow. It was, he told the British Council of Shopping Centres in 1990, "not just a new product launch; it was a social and cultural event of international proportions." While others were thinking about the peace dividend at the end of the cold war or about the triumph of democracy, he was thinking about the beginning of global marketing and the arrival of the new, placeless consumer, belonging to a world where allegiances to brand names have replaced the more dangerous and visceral loyalties of history and geography.

He looks and sounds like a man who has made a nonsense of history, and indeed of geography. His deep voice carries an Irish accent that has been levelled out by a quarter of a century in America so that it seems to echo with only the faintest undertone of time and place. His easy mimicry, the way he slips, in his jokes, into perfectly tuned Belfast or Dublin, or English or American accents, serves merely to emphasise the neutrality of his own voice, to draw attention to the fact that local inflections are something he can put on, or take off, at will. And everything he is saying seems to suggest that he really believes that history is over, that the business of the world, now and forever more, is business.

But something, perhaps the fact that he is speaking in a hotel that was known until recently, in spite of the antiseptic internationalism of its decor, as the most bombed building in Europe, seems suddenly to make him doubtful. History did not really end, he muses. It "emerged from the permafrost of communism. Theological nationalism is re-emerging." It is an anomalous moment of doubt, and it passes quickly. He moves on to talk with his usual certainty about the scarce and demanding nature of capital, about the need to get governments off the back of business, about the beneficial effects of the North American Free Trade Agreement in allowing Heinz to keep wages down. But somehow, the moment lingers as an undercurrent of fear. Even Tony O'Reilly can't mention theological nationalism in Belfast without reminding his audience that there are other forces in the world besides global competition. And even he knows, from his own life, something about those forces.

Had any of the businessmen at that conference in Belfast been present in November, 1982 at a function in the Abbey Theatre to honour Peadar O'Donnell, they would have been amazed to find Tony O'Reilly not merely present, but more or less running the show. O'Donnell embodied in many ways a past that few of them would have wanted to recognise. As well as being a distinguished novelist, he was also the last surviving member of the executive of the old IRA. He was an old Marxist radical, a fiery trade union organiser and professional agitator. And he was, for five years in the late 1940s and early 1950s, Tony O'Reilly's mentor. When O'Reilly started his tribute to O'Donnell by declaring that the old man had "almost reared me", many of those present thought, at first, that it was another of O'Reilly's jokes, that the punchline would be coming soon.

There was no punchline. O'Donnell's nephew and namesake was O'Reilly's best friend at school, and the two spent all their summers in O'Donnell's big house in the countryside near Dungloe in County Donegal. "Peadar was Uncle Peadar to me", O'Reilly told his audience, "and his wife was Auntie Lil... I remember Peadar's glittering conversation and the notion that we were both interested in Marx; he in Karl, I in Groucho." The predictable joke, intended to dismiss the strangeness of this icon of multinational capitalism adopting a Communist uncle, could not hide the vestiges of rapture in the memory of golden times: "I learned how to fish there, how to row, and how to drink altar wine." Those, he recalled, were "sunlit days, and both glittering and glamorous as well." For once, he had nothing clever to say, no pronouncements to make. For once, he allowed the distance between the president of Heinz and a certain kind of Irish past to stretch over a terrain not of triumph but of loss.

O'Donnell was just one of three veterans of Ireland's bloody wars who helped to shape O'Reilly's early life, and the memory of the other two was less golden. When he was born in 1936, in a state still struggling to emerge from the bloody circumstances of its birth, Tony O'Reilly was named after his mother's brother, Tony O'Connor, who was always to be his favourite uncle. Uncle Tony was a man who had seen history at first hand. In the savage civil war that followed the Anglo-Irish treaty of 1921, fought between those who accepted the establisment of an Irish Free State within the British Empire, and those who wanted to hold out for a republic, the O'Connors took the Free State side. One of their cousins commanded the firing squad that executed the novelist and former clerk of the House of Commons, Erskine Childers, who fought on the republican side. Tony O'Connor himself joined the Free State army when it was established, and, before he was twenty, he had "killed at least a dozen fellow Irishmen in the wild country-road skirmishes" that constituted the civil war, rising in the process to the rank of sergeant.

He survived the war, but he was always haunted by the memory of a day in January 1923 in the barracks in Athlone, where he grew up and played as a child with a "tall, slender and dark-haired" boy whom he later called Johnny. For over 50 years, he carried with him the secret of what had happened to Johnny that day. In 1975, when his favourite nephew had ascended beyond the internecine hatreds of a small nation, and was already president and chief executive of H.J. Heinz, he let the secret out.

His nephew had by then reached a point from which he could look back on Irish history, with all its immemorial entanglements, as a joke. In 1970, for instance, when he was managing director of Heinz UK, he had made an extraordinary comeback, after an absence of 15 years, to the Irish rugby team playing England at Twickenham. In the programme for the match, he wrote a burlesque of Anglo-Irish history in which even the massacres of Cromwell could be laughed about: "To the English it is a game of rugger — to the Irish an historical pageant, the continuation of centuries of loose rucks, crooked into the scrum, and bad refereeing, including a particularly nasty period when England were strong up front and had Oliver C. at fly-half, 'a very mean fella with the boot and elbow and distinctly anti-clerical when he got you on the ground', as a decaying Irish wing-forward was heard to remark."

For his uncle, though, history was not a game, but a personal burden, a story he would like to forget but was compelled to remember. Even then, it was too painful to be told bluntly and was wrapped in a thin layer of fiction, as a novel called *He's Somewhere In There*. Its status, though, was deliberately confused in a foreword confessing that the story, in spite of its fictional form, was "a factual account of the Western Sector during the Irish Civil War."

If the line between fact and fiction is unclear, so too is that between history and news. The memories of bloody death that came spilling out between the covers of the book had an awful familiarity in 1975, in the middle of the worst period of sectarian murder in the Northern Ireland conflict. The sense of violence as a cycle, an inescapable undertow, even "a way of life", is continually present in Tony O'Connor's memory, and he has his fictional *alter ego* remark to himself that "ancient hates and mediaeval-thinking churchmen would ensure another flare-up in the not-too-distant future. I'd be far better to get the hell out of it." The pressure of the day's newspapers can be felt in every line, squeezing out an old man's confession that what is happening now has all happened before.

What he remembered most vividly was death: "I bent over Jim Balfe, my room-mate, lying in a pool of black liquid. His head was twisted by his left shoulder, severed but for a piece of skin, which seemed reluctant to let it go. I shuddered. God almighty! He was alive a few seconds ago! As gently as I could, I eased the cold, sightless head back to the bloodied stump of a neck. He seemed whole again. When I stood up, I knew I was going to be sick, but Sergeant Madigan quietened my retching stomach with a quick, sharp yell..."

What he wanted to recount most urgently, though, was his own intimate betrayal of his friend Johnny. He and Johnny were neighbours and best friends. Johnny joined the IRA and when the truce with the British was declared, emerged from the undergound as a glamorous hero.

Wanting to be like him, Tony joined the new national army. As soon as he was in, the army split, and Johnny disappeared into the diehard faction, leaving Tony behind, caught in a nightmare of carnage.

After seven months of war, his comrades brought in six captured republicans, Johnny among them, and decided to shoot them. Tony was forced to watch as his friend was killed, afraid to speak or to plead: "Through a mist of tears I tried hard to restrain, I looked over at Johnny with the life gone out of him. Those gay eyes would smile no more and he would be buried in a lost grave thirty yards from the handball alley where we had played so often."

He was haunted ever afterwards, not just by the deed, but by its secrecy: "Only those involved would know they were gone. There would be no listings in daily orders, no newspaper reports. It could be months or years before relations heard what had happened to their rebel husbands or sons. Talk was dangerous, and the men who were unlucky enough to form part of any firing party were always given separate, speedy postings to various camps around the country. Even then, one careless slip would result in them being trailed and a bullet-ridden body found in a ditch."

When Johnny's mother came to ask about her son, Tony said nothing, but his older self, looking back across a gap of 50 years, reflects that Johnny will be there forever: "Forever and forgotten, like those with him will be forgotten. They fought for a cause that failed, and how it failed! And they will be forgotten because Ireland, in its own shame, cannot afford to remember them."

By the time the book appeared, his nephew, Tony O'Reilly, already controlled Independent Newspapers, the largest newspaper group in Ireland. The book's oblique commentary on news — on the force of facts that do not appear in the newspapers, on the way today's news headlines are yesterday's dark secrets, on the things that societies cannot afford to remember and speak about —

must have struck O'Reilly with peculiar force. All the more so because he had his own intimate secrets of subterfuge and betrayal to protect.

In March 1987, Tony O'Reilly handed over a piece of England to Margaret Thatcher. Having bought Cape Cornwall, a mile of English coastline, he presented it to Mrs Thatcher at a public ceremony, remarking as he did so that it was especially *piquant* that an Irishman should be presenting the title deeds for a piece of "English land" to a British prime minister and that he did so with a special sense of privilege. It was an odd but telling moment, a half-comic, half-serious reversal of those poignant end-of-empire scenes like the surrender of Dublin Castle to Michael Collins in 1922 or the handing over of Irish ports to Eamon de Valera in 1939, when Tony O'Reilly was a small child. It was an act of historic cheek, but also an act of great confidence, a public sign that here was an Irishman who didn't have to watch out for himself in England.

A moment that helps to explain it is one that happened on a night during the second world war. Brendan Bracken, the British Minister for Information, was introduced at the Ritz to Major-General Emmet Dalton, like Tony O'Connor a veteran of the Irish civil war. It was ostensibly an encounter between a successful Englishman and an Irishman who had taken arms against England. When he had stood, successfully, as Tory candidate for North Paddington in 1929, Bracken had described himself in the local papers as being "of Anglo-Irish stock... born in Bedfordshire nearly thirty years ago. He has residences in North Street, Westminster, and in Bedfordshire, Scotland and Ireland. He graduated at Oxford University." He was, in other words, exactly the sort of person who might own, as he did, a controlling interest in *The Economist* and *The Financial Times*.

But Dalton recognised Bracken and said to Lord Milton, who was introducing them, that "Brendan and I know one another of old. We were schoolmates in Dublin." Bracken tried to look puzzled. How could a wealthy Bedfordshire man of Anglo-Irish stock have been to school with a lower middle-class Irish rebel? Dalton became angry. "If you don't remember me, Brendan," he said, "I bloody well remember you and those corduroy trousers which you wore day in day out until you stank to high heaven. The smell is not out of my nostrils yet."

Bracken was the most spectacular example of what an Irishman had once had to do if he wanted to be an English press baron. Brought up Catholic and Irish in Dublin, the son of a Fenian revolutionary, he re-invented himself as an English toff. When he first arrived in England, he pretended to be Australian, then enrolled himself in a public school to learn the right manners and accent. He stayed in Oxford for a while, so that he could subsequently pass himself off as a graduate of Balliol. And he acquired for himself a set of impeccably Tory and imperialist views, impressing Winston Churchill as a soul-mate and indispensable ally.

The problem with such a feat of camouflage, though, was that it entailed a constant risk of exposure. The power involved in being the owner of newspapers was limited by the possibility of being a victim of newspapers. In 1944, Beaverbrook sent a reporter to Ireland to uncover Bracken's true background. Bracken used his powers as Minister for Information to excise references to his father's record as an Irish rebel from the *Evening Standard*. Even so, there were always people like Dalton who knew him when his trousers stank to high heaven.

When, in a dawn raid in early 1994, Tony O'Reilly bought 25 per cent of Newspaper Publishing, publishers of the London *Independent* and *Independent on Sunday*, he became the first Irishman since Bracken to own a large chunk of an English media group. As a keen reader of English history, he knew enough about his predecessor to recognise the similarities between himself and Bracken.

Like O'Reilly, Bracken came from a family with a strong connection to Irish nationalist history. Like him, he grew up in the Catholic middle-class suburbs of North Dublin. Like him, he was educated by Irish Jesuits. And like Bracken, O'Reilly idolised Winston Churchill.

Bracken's connection with Churchill was so strong that it was widely, though falsely, believed that he was the Prime Minister's natural son. O'Reilly's connection was second-hand and imaginary. Churchill was his "great hero", and he quoted him regularly in his speeches. "His life to me", O'Reilly once told the BBC, "was and continues to be an inspiration." Asked what he had taken from Churchill he replied that "I think he was a very selfish man. He believed he was the epicentre of all that was happening. He was... a truly conceited man. He felt he was very important, and I suppose that is one of the principle criteria of success — to believe in yourself so strongly that you are the epicentre of all that is happening."

O'Reilly could, indeed, have been a milder version of Bracken. The rugby writer Terry Maclean, covering the Lions rugby tour of New Zealand in 1959, noted O'Reilly's attitude to those English members of the side who came from upper-class backgrounds. It was, he wrote, "a strange regard, almost amounting to envy, for those fortunate folk who move through the world with a lordly calm based upon a secure place in the scheme of things." His idolisation of Churchill, his avid reading of biographies of other British prime ministers like Disraeli and Gladstone, his adoption of the style of a lord of the manor in his Georgian mansion at Castlemartin in County Kildare, all bear witness to that strange regard. When the band played *Land of Hope and Glory* as he entered the village hall in Kilcullen, near Castlemartin, for his vast 50th birthday party, it was not an entirely inappropriate anthem.

But O'Reilly never had the opportunity that Bracken had to re-invent himself as someone else. His rugby career made him a star before he was 20, a visible international symbol of Ireland. Disguise, even had he wanted it, was impossible for a red-haired boy in a green shirt, ducking and weaving before cheering crowds. And besides, Tony O'Reilly had darker, more intimate secrets to conceal than Brendan Bracken ever had. Disguise invites revelation, and early in his career, Tony O'Reilly was terribly vulnerable to revelations.

When he was 17, Tony O'Reilly discovered that he was not, as he had always believed, an only child. In his last year at school, one of the Jesuit priests who taught him took him aside and told him that his parents were not married, that his father had another wife and other children, that he himself had three half-sisters and a half-brother whom he had never seen. The priest may have told him all of this because he wanted to spare him the shock of later revelations, or he may have been concerned that Tony might be considering, as most bright Irish boys did at some stage, entering the priesthood. An illegitimate child, which is what he was, could not be a priest.

That rule reflected a wider prejudice in an overhwhelmingly Catholic society obsessed with sexual purity. The playwright Hugh Leonard, who grew up illegitimate in the Dublin of the 1930s and 1940s, "knew that to be what they called illegitimate was an occasion for deep shame. There had been a sin of some kind, and because of it you were not the same as children who had parents. I had heard neighbours and ladies in the town tell this to my mother, not in so many words, but by some pitying murmurs... accompanied by a movement of the hand which made to touch my hair, but desisted just in time. My mother would not dare to defend bastardy; instead she behaved like a woman whose child is known to have committed murder, but who against all reason declares him innocent."

Even in the early 1960s, an American Jesuit researching attitudes in Ireland found that the general belief was that "illegitimate babies are bad, bad, bad." Just five years before Tony O'Reilly was born, the Irish state made it explictly clear that illegitimate children were, in the eyes of the law, second class. The Legitimacy Act of 1931 allowed, grudgingly, that a child born out of wedlock might inherit its mother's property if she died without making a will. But it refused to grant any such rights of succession to the estate of a child's natural father who, was, after all, infinitely more likely to have property and money.

Only when Tony O'Reilly was 28, a famous sportstar and an icon of a changing Ireland, did Irish law give statutory expression to the notion that an unmarried woman had the right to be regarded as the guardian of her child. Even then, the stigma of illegitimacy retained the sanction of law. As late as 1985, the Irish Supreme Court ruled that children born out of wedlock had no rights of succession to their father's estate. Not until 1987 was the legal concept of illegitimacy abolished in Ireland. Well past the age of 50, Tony O'Reilly, as well as being the richest man in Ireland was also, secretly, a second-class Irishman.

Tony O'Reilly's position was in one sense less shameful than that of the child of an ordinary unmarried mother: he was cherished and recognised by both his natural parents. But in another sense it was more darkly secretive. For most illegitimate children, the sin was acknowledged and open, the shame explicit. There was, at least, little else to be revealed. But for him, his public identity was a subterfuge. His parents pretended to be married, and concealed the existence of a whole other family. His cupboard contained, not a skeleton, but several living reminders of what was being hidden: his half-siblings. Not only was the existence of his father's other family a secret, but so was the fact that he himself knew about it. He told neither his father nor his mother that he shared their private knowledge until the early 1970s. For twenty more years after that, until he allowed his official biographer Ivan Fallon to reveal the truth, he watched as every profile of him in a magazine or newspaper around the world repeated the official lie that he was an only child.

No one can ever know how much their inner lives are shaped by social circumstances, and no one else can ever guess. But it is hard to avoid the belief that something of his anomalous origins must be present in what Tony O'Reilly has become. It may be there in the obsessive, driven hunger for success that is evident in the career of a man who could not be content with being one the highest paid managers in America but has also used his spare time to build a private industrial empire and to pursue the dream of being a global media mogul. It may be there in the attitude to Ireland, that peculiar mixture of distance from a society and intimate knowledge of its workings that belongs to a secret outsider who looks like the ultimate insider. And it must be there in the overwhelming desire to control news, to have power over image and information.

If the Ireland that Tony O'Reilly grew up in had any of the tabloid newspapers that Tony O'Reilly now controls — newspapers like the *The Sunday World,* modelled on *The News of the World,* or the Irish edition of *The Star*, which he controls jointly with the Express group — they would certainly have revealed his secrets. Because of rugby, he was famous as a schoolboy, a glamorous public figure, fair game for prurient curiosity. If, at any time in his youth, his family background had been revealed, it would have caused not just personal hurt but probably fatal damage to his public career. His success depended on media reticence, on the maintenance of a clear distinction between the private realm and the public.

Equally, in 1962, when O'Reilly was head of the Irish Milk Marketing Board, and his car hit a cyclist as he was driving back to Dublin from a rugby match, his father was able to arrange to have to incident kept quiet, and no newspaper reported it, even though he was one of the best-known men in Ireland. In the most intimate way imaginable, he learned the meaning of news. He learned that news is also about what is not said, and that the ability to control what can and cannot be said about you is an indispensible form of power. For such a man, the ownership of newspapers would always be more than a business.

Yet none of this has had any discernible effect on his attitude to news values, and his tabloid papers have been no better, if no worse, than those belonging to Rupert Murdoch, whom he affects to regard as a barbarian at the gates. He publicly defended the *Sunday World*, for instance, when some Independent Newspapers shareholders attacked it at the company's AGM. One of them complained particularly about an article about female bus conductors in Dublin, then a new phenomenon and an important test-case for women in traditionally male roles, which appeared under the headline "Randy Clippies". It was, the shareholder said, "a cheap and scurrilous attack on the sexual morality of an easily identified small group of women in this city." O'Reilly told him, though, that "just because of the somewhat prurient nature of some of its publications", there was no reason why the *Sunday World* should not be part of the group. "In many cases", he remarked, "we try to lead public taste, but in most we follow it."

In April 1993, his *Sunday Independent* ran what purported to be an interview with Bishop Eamon Casey, who had fled Ireland after admitting that he was the father of a child. If it had indeed taken place, the interview would have been a world-wide scoop. But in fact, as the paper subsequently admitted, it had not taken place. O'Reilly, asked about this, merely said that he was "out of the country" when the story ran and that he had not read it or been briefed by his executives about it before it appeared. He wasn't, he said, involved in making editorial decisions "in that way".

But he is certainly involved in other ways. Sixty in 1996, and likely to retire from Heinz soon, Tony O'Reilly has chosen to devote his old age not to the racehorses which his second wife Chryss Goulandris, a member of a hugely wealthy Greek shipping dynasty, raises on their estate at Castlemartin, or to a prestigious company like Waterford Wedgewood (makers of Waterford crystal and Wedgewood china), which he controls, but to making himself a global media mogul. In 1973, he bought control of Independent Newspapers in Dublin for just £1 million. The company now has assets of £500 million, and effectively controls businesses worth £1 billion. Slowly at first and then quite suddenly, Independent Newspapers has expanded beyond Ireland and into Britain, France, Portugal, Mexico, South Africa, Australia and New Zealand. Between 1994 and 1996, Independent has acquired 60 per cent of the Argus group, South Africa's largest newspaper chain (of which his official biographer Ivan Fallon is now editorial director), 43 per cent of Newspaper Publishing in Britain, 55 per cent of Australian Provincial Newspapers, 25 per cent of Irish Press Newspapers in Ireland, and 44 per cent of Wilson and Horton, the largest newspaper group in New Zealand. It also has extensive interests in cable television in Ireland, radio and television in Australia, and outdoor advertising in Portugal, France and Mexico. And it is clear that O'Reilly intends to expand his empire: he tried to buy the Fairfax group in Australia, but lost out to Conrad Black, and has made little secret of his interest in both the Mirror and Express groups in Britain.

He has always claimed that "I have never sought to exercise any personal political power in the newspapers." Guarantees of editorial independence were an important part of his failed bid for the Fairfax group in Australia in 1991, and of his attempt to acquire Newspaper Publishing in Britain. But he does hold a three-day strategy meeting every year which his editors as well as his managers are expected to attend. And he talks on the phone every day to Independent's deputy chairman, John Meagher.

Even though O'Reilly does not interfere directly in the content of the newspapers he owns, nobody seriously doubts that his influence, however passive, is pervasive. He failed to convince the Competition Authority in Ireland that his company could have a majority stake in a newspaper, in this case the *Sunday Tribune,* without limiting its editorial independence. The authority was shown a quotation from O'Reilly, based on the style-book of the *Washington Post*, of which he was then a director, in which he stated that "In a world where the ownership of newspapers is increasingly concentrated amongst a smaller group of names... the newspaper's duty is to its readers and to the public at large and not to the private interests of the owner." It was also told that Independent Newspapers had agreed an editorial charter for the *Tribune* guaranteeing editorial independence. But it was unconvinced by either of these submissions.

In refusing him permission to take a majority stake in *The Sunday Tribune*, the Competition Authority pointed out that his proposal for an editorial charter would have little real effect: "There would not seem to be a possibility... that an editor could be completely independent of the proprietor of the paper, and it seems unlikely that this could ever be properly established. At the end of the day, the editor is constrained by commercial and financial considerations, which can be conclusive. The editor may exercise self-censorship, deliberately or unconsciously. There may be direct interference by the proprietor, or influence may be imposed in more subtle ways, and an editor may take heed of the proprietor for fear of losing his job." In fact, in early 1994, Independent's two directors on the *Tribune* board supported a successful motion to sack the paper's editor Vincent Browne, who had attacked the *Suinday Independent* in print over the Bishop Casey affair.

In spite of such concerns, Tony O'Reilly has now reached a position in Ireland where, as the Competition Authority expressed it in 1995, in another report on his dealings —

this time his investments in the rival *Irish Press* group —
"the possibility cannot be ruled out that in a relatively
short period of time, the only remaining Irish newpapers
would be those owned in whole or in part by Independent
Newspapers plc." The authority found, in this instance,
that O'Reilly's investments in the *Irish Press*, which closed
in 1995, was made to prevent it being taken over by
another newspaper group "which might be expected to
compete more vigorously in the market for newspapers
and newspapers advertising." The rhetoric of free market
competition that trips so easily off his lips is somewhat
undermined by the authority's finding that his *Irish Press*
investment "amounts to an abuse of a dominant position"
in the marketplace.

✦ ✦ ✦ ✦ ✦

The complex relationship between politics, money and
the control of newspapers that O'Reilly embodies is best
illustrated in the hysteria over oil exploration off the coast
of Ireland in the 1980s. In the middle years of that decade,
as the economic boom of the 1960s and early 1970s turned
to bust, the rural poor turned for salvation to the Blessed
Virgin and the urban rich to Tony O'Reilly. While the
national debt rose beyond £20 billion, and the rate of
unemployment went beyond 20 per cent, while all the
country's dreams of prosperous modernity turned sour,
ordinary people in rural Ireland started to see statues of
the Virgin moving, waving, weeping, floating. But while
the doctors and dentists, the solicitors and small
businessmen of the cities sneered at them, they, too, looked
to their own icon to perform a miracle. Instead of prayers
and candles, they laid share certificates at the feet of
Anthony John Francis O'Reilly.

Such was the charisma, the allure, the sheer magic of
O'Reilly's name, that at his call Irish investors poured £50
million into five deep holes in the Atlantic seabed, off the
coast of County Waterford, into which O'Reilly himself put

£5 million of his own money. The oil crisis of 1979 had sent the Irish economy into a downward spiral, and they believed with all their hearts that Tony O'Reilly would find oil under the sea and save the nation. When Atlantic Resources made its shares available on the Dublin stock market in April, 1981 there were, as all the newspapers agreed, "unprecedented scenes of mayhem". Throughout the mid-1980s, there were bouts of hysterical exultation and suicidal depression as the price of shares in his oil company, Atlantic Resources, fluctuated wildly with every stray rumour caught in the nets of newsprint. The prices of the shares depended on speculation in the newspapers, and Tony O'Reilly owned many of them.

There was more than money at stake. Oil would save Ireland from debt and allow it to take its place in the Reagan-Thatcher revolution. Thatcher, O'Reilly mused, had used the revenues from North Sea oil to "purchase the silence of the non-working classes". If he, too, struck oil, it would "enable us to pay the bill, as it has enabled Mrs Thatcher to pay the bill while she put into effect the structural changes that are going on in Britain".

The oil rush could not be disentangled from O'Reilly's position as the owner of many Irish newspapers. In a rare moment of genuine indiscretion, he told *Forbes* magazine in September 1983 that his geologist had chosen six blocks of seabed for exploration. "Since I own 35 per cent of the newspapers in Ireland I have close contact with the politicians. I got the blocks he wanted."

Even after he got those blocks, however, O'Reilly became increasingly impatient with what he saw as the restrictive terms imposed by the Irish government in its exploration licences. Garret FitzGerald, who headed that government for most of the period, had been a friend of O'Reilly's since the early 1960s, but he felt the effects of O'Reilly's anger.

O'Reilly had supported FitzGerald's liberal, mildly social democratic politics, and, according to FitzGerald, "once he acquired Independent Newspapers, he remained very supportive". In 1982, when Charles Haughey was in power and there were allegations that his government was interfering with the independence of the police, FitzGerald "was in touch with" O'Reilly "over the political situation". "In talking to him over that period it was kind of on the assumption that he had some degree of influence over the newspapers, I suppose. I certainly would have been seeking his assistance, in terms of the papers at that time. If I was ringing him, it wasn't just for a general chat."

"When we were in government", he recalls, "he remained supportive to a degree, but towards the end there's no doubt that the Independent swung somewhat, and I think the oil thing was a major factor. He felt that the terms we were imposing for oil were too tough and he wanted them changed, and I must say that I thought they were too tough. The pressure was expressed rationally enough in terms of the need to modify the terms. I didn't feel there was improper pressure. But I felt as time went on, he was getting more and more frustrated, and he was allowing this to influence his overall judgement. He became irritable, and angry. And I didn't think he was very helpful to us afterwards as a result. I have no complaints about that, but our relationship never recovered."

There is a sense in which Tony O'Reilly has always been in media, even when he was not yet in the newspaper business. He is a self-made man, a folk hero of capitalism who has built a personal fortune of £500 million from a standing start. But he is a hero of capitalism's unheroic age. His genius is not for making or inventing things, but for buying cheap and selling hard.

Though he heads a great industrial enterprise, his interest is not really in manufacturing at all. In 1986, for instance, he threatened, somewhat rhetorically, to take Heinz out of manufacturing altogether, to buy its food products from factories who could produce them cheaply, and to concentrate instead on selling brands and tastes. He is part of an age of capitalism in which the idea of the

the entrepreneur as inventor is long past. As a multinational manager he does essentially two things — he cuts costs and he buys companies. One of his most famous ideas at Heinz was that of taking the back label off the ketchup bottle, saving $4 million a year. And he has never pretended to be interested in developing new things to sell. He told New York journalists in 1978 that "The best way to get into new product development is to steal the other guy's ideas. You buy the company." This essentially is what he does.

Having bought or made the products, he turns them into images. In the last financial year, Heinz, under Tony O'Reilly, sold $8 billion worth of food. To do so, it spent $1.7 billion, nearly a quarter of what it earned from sales, on advertising and marketing.

His gift is not so much for thinking up ideas as for selling ideas. As early as 1966, he was saying things like "the greatest supermarket in the world is in the United Kingdom housewife's *mind*". He sells into the supermarket of the mind, stocking its shelves with images and desires. He has come to believe deeply in the magic of brands, in brand-names as a replacement for politics and religion. "Truly great brands", he told the British Council of Shopping Centres in 1990, "are far more than just labels for products; they are symbols that encapsulate the desires of consumers; they are standards held aloft under which the masses congregate."

His first and most enduring feat of marketing was to turn Ireland itself into a symbol of desire. In 1962, when he was just 26, he was appointed general manager of Bord Bainne, the Irish milk marketing board. The appointment of a dashing young sportsman to such a post was itself heavily symbolic. The nationalist dream of economic and cultural self-sufficiency had finally collapsed under the weight of mass emigration. Fianna Fail, the ruling nationalist party, had abandoned protectionism and invited American multinational companies to invest in

Ireland and engineer a belated industrial revolution in a country that was still overwhelmingly rural and traditional.

The atmosphere was not unlike that of Eastern Europe after the fall of Communism. O'Reilly's appointment coincided with a number of other signals of change: the IRA's abandonment of a violent campaign for a United Ireland, the inauguration of an Irish television service, Ireland's application to join the EEC. The Taoiseach, Sean Lemass gave a speech urging older company directors to "consider whether they have not outlived their usefulness and decide to pass their responsibilities over to younger men." Tony O'Reilly, the most spectacular example of what Lemass desired, was thus himself a kind of symbol, an image of a new Ireland. And this, throughout the rest of his career, is what he has tried to be.

It is this desire that lies behind his refusal to be happy even with his spectacular success at Heinz. Being the bean baron is all very well, but he actually sees himself as very much more than an exemplar of the American corporate dream. He wants to be, at the same time, the embodiment of an Ireland different to that of his adoptive uncle Peadar O'Donnell and his real uncle Tony O'Connor. He wants to be a new Irish brand-name, a standard held aloft under which the masses of Irish around the world can congregate, to be, in his own words, "a representative of the hopes and dreams and aspirations of the Irish around the globe", the man who "planted the flag of the New Ireland abroad in various forms — Independent Newspapers, capitalism, entrepreneurial spirit, managerial competence... The New Ireland which sees we have a right not just to be colonised, but to go to other countries and to harvest and prosper there."

His position in Bord Bainne was a job of considerable political and economic importance: nearly a third of the Irish workforce was employed in agriculture, and what O'Reilly did would directly affect about half a million people from a population of less than three million. What he did was to invent, at the same time as he was inventing himself as a symbol of a new Ireland, a symbol of Irish agriculture that could be marketed firstly in Britain and then around the world: Kerrygold. The product was basic and simple, and he did nothing to change it. It was the wrapping that turned it into money: a name that had, as the marketing reports put it, "a definite Irish sound, with overtones of richness and purity".

In Ireland, the name sounded like nonsense, since Kerry was associated with stony mountains, not green pastures. The satiric novelist Flann O'Brien attacked it in his column in *The Irish Times:* "I have taken care not to inquire as to the names of the persons who constitute this Board, but I'm prepared to go bail there is a preponderance of small, dark men with wiry hair, gnarled features, slightly bandy legs, each with 17 three-act plays stuffed in the old chest in the bedroom: in other words, Kerrymen." But soon Irish people too were buying Kerrygold. The golden wrapping, the sonorous name, turned slabs of butter into desirable objects. The allure of the image, the magic of brands, had been released into an emerging Ireland, and Tony O'Reilly was the conjurer.

The old history, the old Ireland, could not be transformed so easily, though. Moving on from Bord Bainne after his triumph with Kerrygold, he was appointed by the Irish government to head an even bigger state enterprise, the Irish Sugar Company. He replaced the third veteran of the nationalist struggle, and of the civil war, to play a part in Tony O'Reilly's career, General Michael Costello.

In the official summary of his career prepared by Tony O'Reilly's press agent, all the many companies in which he has played a leading role are listed — except one. H.J. Heinz is there of course, as are Independent Newspapers, his investment conglomerate Fitzwilton, Waterford Wedgewood, the minerals and oil company Arcon, Bord Bainne and the Irish Sugar Company. The one exception is Erin Foods. It is easy to understand the omission: Erin is a sensitive subject. But equally, it is hard to understand O'Reilly's career unless you understand what happened to Erin.

Costello was a veteran of the old IRA, a protege of Michael Collins, who promoted him from private to Colonel Commandant at the age of 18 after a particularly daring operation during the civil war, in which he took the Free State side. Afterwards he became a general, then the head of the Irish Sugar Company, a large nationalised industry which processed sugar beet. He brought the charisma of history and a military attention to detail to the job. More importantly, he applied the idealism of the first generation of nationalist revolutionaries, a deep belief in co-operative effort, in self-reliance and in public service. He came to hate O'Reilly, and, with time, the feeling became mutual.

Costello was fiercely anti-communist, but he was also, almost as passionately, anti-capitalist. He saw "co-operation" as the "only alternative to the Communist collective or the amalgamation of small farms to form large capitalistic enterprises." And he tried to create an aggressively commercial but socially progressive food processing industry in rural Ireland, by setting up a company called Erin Foods (Erin means, simply, Ireland, and the symbolism was intentional — Costello saw the company as a national metaphor) as a subsidiary of Irish Sugar. A team of young scientists in Irish Sugar had developed a new freeze-drying technology, which meant that vegetables could be packed, stored outside a fridge (still a rare enough appliance) and reconstituted simply by pouring boiling water over them. Costello intended to use it to sell the produce of Irish agricultural co-operatives and state-owned factories, first to Irish cities and then to the huge British market. To do this he would have to take on the dominant companies in the British processed food market — among them Heinz.

One of Costello's most important allies was an extraordinary Catholic priest, James McDyer. Mc Dyer, a radical socialist in clerical clothing, had founded a rural commune in a poor and remote part of County Donegal, Glencolumbkille, and with the encouragement and support of Peadar O'Donnell, he persuaded Costello to site one of his vegetable processing factories there. Costello, as Brendan Halligan, a young economist with Erin in the 1960s, recalls "dreamed of creating a network of factories, to bring about the stablilisation of population in rural areas. He was motivated by old fashioned nationalism — wanting to develop the economy, seeing resources lying unused, and being extremely angry about that, and seeing the depopulation of large parts of the country. He embarked on the Erin dream without the civil service in the Department of Finance or the political establishment really understanding what he was at. When he got to a certain point and he was investing a lot of money which they regarded as losses, they began to understand." And when they understood what he was doing, they moved to stop him.

In December, 1966 Costello left Irish Sugar and Erin Foods and recommended, in his letter of resignation, that "someone be found who believes that food processing can be run as the Department of Finance wants it run." That someone was Tony O'Reilly . He was given the job by the leading Fianna Fail politicians Jack Lynch and Charles Haughey, and by the Department of Finance, which had long distrusted Costello's tendency to put social objectives on the same plane as commercial ones. Officially, O'Reilly was said to be continuing Costello's work, with a brief "to build the marketing structure that would enable a big expansion to take place in the export drive". The government assured parliament that "Erin Foods is now engaged in a vigorous development of the UK market and an expansion of their existing range of products." In fact, his job was to cut back the operation, stop Erin from competing with private enterprise, and tidy up its chaotic books.

Within a month, O'Reilly was in touch with Heinz, one of Erin's competitors, to offer a deal. The two companies would merge. Erin would supply Heinz with raw vegetables for processing, and would itself sell Heinz products in Ireland. The Erin offices in Britain would close, and its sales force would be sacked. Two Heinz executives would sit on the Erin board. As for Peadar O'Donnell and James McDyer, they would have to realise that, as O'Reilly later told his official biographer, "You just can't grow vegetables competitively on the hillsides of Donegal". O'Reilly and Haughey, now Minister for Finance, on a winter holiday together in the Canaries, discussed the deal, and Haughey was pleased.

Shortly after the deal went through, and the new company Heinz-Erin was formed, O'Reilly addressed the workers and small farmers of Glencolumbkille and warned them that they must "appreciate that the international marketplace is the supreme discipline in their activities. Heinz-Erin provides such a challenge."

To Costello, the deal was a "give-away". He maintained until his death in 1986 that Erin "had Heinz beaten as competitors", and that "Heinz certainly got more out of the deal than Erin Foods, even to the extent of buying Irish vegetables in bulk and shipping them out to factories in Britain where they provide employment which could be better provided here." He revealed that Heinz had already offered a merger while he was in charge, and that he had rejected it "out of hand" — "Heinz were simply like other foreign firms, looking for something for nothing, or something for very little, anyway. In fact they got something for nothing. Nobody had anything to gain in this country, but naturally enough the people who delivered to Heinz had a lot to gain."

For Tony O'Reilly, the deal was the beginning of his global career. Less than two years after he joined Irish

Sugar and Erin, O'Reilly was negotiating a job with Heinz and in May 1969, became managing director of Heinz UK. Two years after that, he was in Pittsburgh as senior vice-president, and by 1973 he was president and chief operating officer of Heinz worldwide.

Erin, meanwhile, dwindled slowly towards death. The merger with Heinz was a commercial failure, and O'Reilly left the company in poor shape. It stumbled on for years as an agency for Heinz in Ireland. In 1990, Heinz, of which Tony O'Reilly was now chairman, president and chief executive, announced abruptly that it was planning to remove the sale and marketing of its products in Ireland from Erin Foods. Erin's chief executive told the press that "I'm extremely disappointed in Tony O'Reilly. I thought Tony had more loyalty to the business." Tony O'Reilly was unavailable for comment, even to his own newspapers.

When Tony O'Reilly moved to Heinz, he made a profound statement about the nature of power in the late twentieth century. For he did so in spite of the fact that he could, at that stage, have launched a political career that would, almost certainly, have taken him all the way to the office of Taoiseach. Given a choice between running a multinational company and running a small European country, he chose the former. He had seen that once Ireland opened itself up to American multinationals, the idea of national sovereignty, of state control, had become untenable. Years later, when idealistic nationalists came to power in Africa, first Robert Mugabe in Zimbabwe, then Nelson Mandela in South Africa, he would point out to them with persuasive force that they could not run their own economies, that economic nationalism was dead, that they would have to come terms with the power of scarce and demanding capital.

Shortly after Mugabe was installed in power in Harare, on a Marxist and nationalist platform, O'Reilly went to see him to try to persuade him to allow Heinz to open a plant there. "We had both been educated by Irish Jesuits", he later recalled, "and through this common kinship, we discussed the notion, the model of economic nationalism...I was trying to teach him about the limits of economic nationalism". His arguments about the nature and limits of political power were persuasive — Heinz and the Zimbabwean state established a profitable joint venture, Olivine.

Equally, in spite of the fact that he had boasted as late as 1988 that, were he still playing rugby, he would play in South Africa, in spite of UN sanctions, and that he would have "immediate access" to old rugby comrades like General Magnus Malan, subsequently acquitted on murder charges arising from his involvement in the establishment of death squads, he quickly established a friendship with Nelson Mandela after the latter's release from prison. Mandela spent the Christmas and New Year of 1993-1994 in O'Reilly's holiday home on the island of Nassau. He, too, came to accept the limits of political power, among them the necessity to allow a foreign businessman like Tony O'Reilly to take over his country's largest newspaper group.

In the late 1960s, O'Reilly himself was offered political power by both of Ireland's major political parties. The Fianna Fail Taoiseach, Jack Lynch, who had sponsored him from the start, told him that if he refused the Heinz job, he would make him Minister for Agriculture in his cabinet. But the rival Fine Gael party also asked him to stand in the 1969 general election. The offer was made by Garret FitzGerald, who says that "I had the authority of the party to talk to him. I wasn't authorised, so far as I can recall, to say to him that he would be a Minister, but he obviously would have had a good prospect of ministerial office given his abilites. But then he got the offer of the Heinz job in England. And he said to me 'Garret, if I get the Heinz job I can make £100,000 clear in five years and come back and enter full time into politics.'"

Fine Gael and Fianna Fail were the political heirs of the two sides in the Irish civil war. The fact that both of them wanted O'Reilly was a sign of how far he had succeeded in creating a persona that transcended history, that seemed finally to lay all the ghosts of the past. In his bright, charming, efficient persona, lay the promise of an end to history, of a politics that would be about management, not ideology. But the paradox of that image is that on the one hand it seemed to offer a new Ireland but on the other it embodied an embrace of the global economy in which no Ireland, new or old, could really matter.

From time to time since he went to Heinz, the idea of a political career for Tony O'Reilly has re-surfaced, but now on a much larger scale than that of Ireland. In 1980, Garret FitzGerald authorised a fresh approach to O'Reilly, testing whether he would agree to stand in the next election. He "quite possibly" would have appointed him to the cabinet. "At that stage, he would have had a reasonable expectation of office, if he was going to divert his whole career from where he was. And he would have been very dynamic I'm sure." But Ireland was now too small a stage. And FitzGerald was subsequently relieved that O'Reilly had not taken up his offer: "He has perhaps come to feel that Tony O'Reilly's interest is Ireland's interest, is the world's interest, the way people do when they get to his stage."

In 1979, O'Reilly speculated that he might seek to be appointed as a Commissioner of the European Community though "not in the near term". In 1988, he fuelled speculation that he would be appointed US Secretary of Commerce by George Bush, for whom he had served as a fundraiser. But at the same time as he was musing in public on what he might do with the job, he was also making it clear that politicians, even members of the American cabinet have too little power to satisfy him. Unlike Silvio Berlusconi who used his control of large sections of the Italian media to gain political power, O'Reilly has a sharp sense that the global business tycoon and the global media mogul have more power than politicians do. He is also the first person to fully understand that the corporate manager and the media magnate can now be one and the same.

This, more than anything else, is what makes him a representative figure of life at the end of the twentieth century. He belongs definitively to the era of post-industrial capitalism in which a product and its image, commodities and the media through which they are sold, have become virtually indistinguishable. It is an era in which, in his own words, "the communications revolution and the convergence of cultures have set the stage for truly global marketing." And in this era, the relationship between business and news is that of a closed circle. The mass media obliterate the distinctions of aspiration and taste inherent in national cultures. This in turn allows the same company to sell the same product in the same packaging everywhere in the world: "Television will further homogenise the cultures of the developed world. It will in turn generate the cosmopolitan aspirations best satisfied by global brands. The capacity for transnational production is available... The final step in the process will be mass communication. And the technology of satellite and cable tv will make that possible." When that happens, the news in the broadest sense will be not just a report of what happens, but an agent for making it happen.

Recently, when Tony O'Reilly took over Waterford Wedgewood, he commissioned market research in the United States, the main market for Waterford Crystal. Its object was to answer one question — did the consumers of crystal know that Waterford is in Ireland? If they did, the workers in the factory had some power. They could remain, as they had been for many years, a radical elite in the Irish workforce, knowing that since Waterford crystal had to come from Waterford, their product was proof against global forces, against the ruthless mobility of capital. If on the other hand they did not, Waterford crystal could just as well come from Poland or Czechoslovakia, where it could be made much more cheaply. Waterford would, in economic terms, have ceased to be a place and become a brand. And the answer that the research provided was that, indeed, very few American consumers associated Waterford with Ireland. It was the news that Tony O'Reilly wanted to hear: that the process of branding Ireland that he had begun over 30 years before had now reached the point where a part of the country had become, finally, no more than a brand, a name without a face, a placeless image, freed at last from history.

Oscar Wilde: Venus In Blue Jeans

Edward Carson: Listen, sir. Here is one of the 'Phrases and Philosophies' which you contributed to this magazine: 'Wickedness is a myth invented by good people to account for the curious attractiveness of others.' You think that true?

Oscar Wilde: I rarely think that anything I write is true.

We do not know quite when the attractions of wickedness first impressed themselves on Oscar Wilde, but his close encounter with Jesse James must have re-inforced it.

On April 11th 1882, a week after the death of the notorious outlaw, the front page of the New York Daily Graphic was given over to a cartoon called "The Apotheosis of Jesse James". It shows an imposing gravestone with the inscription 'Hic Jacet Jesse James. The most renowned murderer and robber of his age. He quickly rose to eminence in his gallant and dangerous profession and his exploits were the wonder and admiration and excited the emulation of the small boys of the period... He was followed to his grave by mourning relatives, hosts of friends, officers of the law, and the reverend clergy who united in paying extraordinary honours to his memory. Go thou and do likewise!' Around the base of the monument, a legion of small boys, each with a pistol, rifle or knife, does homage to the fallen desperado. What Jean Genet will call, in *The Maids,* "the eternal couple of the criminal and the saint", is already joined together in the apotheosis of Jesse James.

The themes of the cartoon — the glamour of wickedness and the corruption of the young — would become, in due course, central to the fate of Oscar Wilde. What the newspaper was noticing was one of the origins of a central aspect of postmodernity — the erasure of the dividing line between fame and infamy. Jesse James ascended into Heaven with all the trappings of the saint. He was betrayed by a friend before being martyred. And, almost immediately after his death, his relics became objects of worship. Just seven days after his killing, the *Missouri Republican* reported thousands of people visiting the house he had occupied in the town of St Joseph. The owner charged an entry fee of ten cents, though the fence and the stables had been mostly demolished by relic hunters who carried away pieces of them to keep as souvenirs. Their reaction to the death of a violent outlaw suggests that already, in the Wild West of the 1880s, fame had become a transcendent quality, over-riding and over-ruling moral and legal distinctions between the good and the bad.

On April 18th, just over two weeks after the execution of James, Oscar Wilde lectured at Tootle's Opera House in St Joseph as part of his American lecture tour. He noted, as he wrote in a letter to Helena Sickert, that "the whole town was mourning over him and buying relics of his house. His door-knocker and dustbin went for fabulous prices, two speculators absolutely came to pistol shots as to who was to have his hearth-brush, the unsuccessful one being, however, consoled by being allowed to purchase the water-butt for the income of an English bishop, while his sole work of art, a chromo-lithograph of the most dreadful kind, of course was sold at a price which in Europe only a Mantegna or an undoubted Titian can command!"

Wilde may have considered his own performance in America to be original, but in fact it was a replay of a familiar role. To take just one example of an educated Irishman arriving on the western frontier to civilise the natives, there is another Oscar and Trinity College Dublin graduate, Oscar J. Goldrick, who electrified the town of Auroria (now Denver) with his arrival in 1858. Goldrick was driving a wagon drawn by oxen whom he instructed in loud Latin and Greek. He was dressed, according to contemporary reports, in 'a shiny plug hat, polished boots, an immaculate linen shirt, lemon-coloured kid gloves, a Prince Albert coat, and a waistcoat embroidered with lilies of the valley, rosebuds, and violets.' With this costume, he attracted attention for his educational mission, and founded a school and a library, the Denver and Auroria Reading Room Association. Though he may not have known it, Wilde did not invent the role of Irish dandy as American reformer.

What he did do, though, was to recreate that role in the dawning age of mass media and advertising. Wilde arrived as an advertisement. He was the 'original' of Reginald Bunthorne in Gilbert and Sullivan's *Patience*, and his lecture tour was conceived as a way of drumming up publicity for the operetta's American production. Wilde was playing a version of a theatrical exaggeration of himself. And, like one of Andy Warhol's paintings of Marilyn Monroe, this 'Oscar Wilde' was itself capable of almost infinite and mechanical reproduction. Before Wilde arrived in Denver in the footsteps of Oscar J. Goldrick, the humorist Eugene Field carried through a successful hoax in which, dressed as 'Oscar Wilde', he was received with ceremony and driven through the streets. Just as versions of Jesse James, and of Billy the Kid, were being 'sighted' all over America, Wilde himself became a transferable icon, an image of dandified civility which was the other side of the coin of the image of outlaw derring-do which attached itself to the notorious desperadoes. Jesse James, Billy the Kid and Oscar Wilde may well be the first human figures to become 'stars' — like Marilyn Monroe — who are themselves commodified and transformed into their own images.

Much later on in Oscar Wilde's career, the shape of these events would become central to his aesthetics. *The Importance of Being Earnest* in particular juggles with roles, with disguises, with the art of the imposter, and with the slipperiness of surface. Wilde's explorations of flatness, depthlessness and superficiality — which cannot but have been influenced by his American experiences — are perhaps the first coherent expression in art of the emergence of a commodified world, a world in which not objects merely but also the human personality can be reproduced and sold in limitless quantity. This is one of the reasons why, in the postmodern culture of the 1990s, Wilde still seems strikingly contemporary.

That Oscar Wilde and Jesse James should have come into such close proximity seems, at first, to fit in well with the official narrative of Wilde's tour of America. He arrived with the mission of civilising America. He was an emissary of the world of civilisation to the world of barbarism. And what could be more demonstrative of the need for such a mission than the Apotheosis of Jesse James? Even to respectable America, the image of a generation of wild children about to be raised on the myth of an outlaw's daring deeds seemed to express its worst nightmares. Wilde's own letter, with its playful comparisons of European culture — which values Mantegna and Titian — and American incivility — which values doorknockers, dustbins and the hideous lithographs of a murderer — is part of the script for that narrative.

Yet if you read on in the same letter, the distinctions begin to blur. Wilde tells how, after St Joseph, he went on to Lincoln, Nebraska, where he lectured to a "charming" audience of university undergraduates. After the lecture, he was driven out to see the State prison: "Poor odd types of humanity in hideous striped dresses making bricks in the sun, and all mean-looking, which consoled me, for I should hate to see a criminal with a noble face. Little whitewashed cells, so tragically tidy, but with books in them. In one I found a translation of Dante, and a Shelley. Strange and beautiful it seemed to me that the sorrow of a single Florentine in exile should, hundreds of years afterwards, lighten the sorrow of some common prisoner in a modern gaol..."

This passage is, of course, among the most haunting that Wilde wrote because we cannot help seeing it as a prefiguration of his own tragedy. Wilde himself stares out at us from prison as a criminal with a noble face. For him too the works of Dante, which he read in their entirety in Reading Gaol, would lighten sorrow. In his own life, he would cease to be the tourist of such places and become the native, cease to be the spectator and become the player. The distinction between civilisation and barbarism, between the artist and the outlaw, on which his American tour is posited, would collapse.

✦ ✦ ✦ ✦ ✦

Carson: Did his rooms strike you as being peculiar?

Wilde: No except that he displayed more taste than usual.

Carson: There was rather elaborate furniture in the rooms, was there not?

Wilde: The rooms were furnished in good taste.

Carson: Is it true that he never admitted daylight into them?

Wilde: Really! I don't know what you mean.

But those distinctions were not, in any case, as rigid as they might have seemed. The behaviour of the mob which flocked to secure the household relics of Jesse James was not all that far removed from the urgings of Oscar Wilde in his lectures to American audiences. One of his lectures was on 'The House Beautiful'. It was concerned with the aesthetics of household furnishings: why wallpaper should not be hung in entrance halls, why heating stoves should be of Dutch porcelain, why secondary colours should be used on walls and ceilings. Why blown glass was to be preferred to cut glass. Making a fetish of domestic goods, giving a charge to everyday objects beyond their functional value, venerating doorknockers and dustbins, was as much a habit of well-to-do consumers as of crazed relic-hunters. For each, functional objects could become imbued with an aura somewhere between the artistic and the religious. Household goods could take on, just as they do in modern advertising, the properties of things touched by magic. They could be, in themselves, suggestive of a moral, or immoral, ambience.

At Wilde's trial, Edward Carson cleverly used the furnishings in the apartment of Alfred Taylor, one of his gay friends, to hint at a whole world of unspeakable decadence. Carson was playing on an obscure but powerful link between criminality and decor, one which was articulated later by Walter Benjamin:

'The furniture style of the second half of the nineteenth century has received its only adequate description and analysis in a certain type of detective novel at the dynamic centre of which stands the horror of apartments. The arrangement of the furniture is at the same time the site plan of deadly traps, and the suite of rooms prescribes the fleeing victim's path. The bourgeois interior of the 1860s to the 1890s, with its gigantic sideboards distended with carvings, the sunless corners where palms stand, the balcony embattled behind its balustrade, and the long corridors with their singing gas flames, fittingly houses only the corpse... The soulless luxuriance of the furnishings becomes true comfort only in the presence of a dead body.'

Nor was the Wilde who passed through Missouri a man entirely outside the world of the outlaw. Outlaw culture was concerned, not merely with violence, but with ways of codifying violence. The Code of the West, by which the likes of Jesse James and Billy the Kid understood themselves to be living, was a code of manners. The outlaw saw himself as a gentlemen. Gentlemen were permitted, as Wilde permitted himself, whoring and carousing and a life beyond the law. But the price for these pleasures was the ability to maintain a disdain for compromise and pragmatic calculation. The code imposed on its followers 'personal courage and pride and reckless disregard of life, it commanded practitioners to avenge all insult and wrong, real or imagined.'

It was, in its own way, a kind of democratised etiquette.

Wilde may have shot from the lip rather than from the hip, and his duels may have been conducted across a dinner table rather than at high noon on a dusty and deserted Main Street, but his public persona had all the hauteur and recklessness of the outlaw. It is well to remember that Wilde's most important predecessor as Irish social comedian in England, Richard Brinsley Sheridan, had to announce his public presence in "society" through two real physical duels, fought against Captain Mathews in Bath and London in 1772. By the time of Wilde's assault on English society, such physical confrontations had been sublimated into wit and dandyism, but the underlying code was little different. In one of his most quoted epigrams — 'My wallpaper and I are fighting a duel to the death; one of us will have to go' — he plays on his own comic transformation of the code of the outlaw into the code of 'taste'. Likewise, in his duel to the death with Carson, his six-gun is loaded with the good taste of the furnishings in a den of iniquity.

And Wilde, of course, came to understand and be fascinated by this connection between the artist and the outlaw in himself. In his essay on the murderer and forger Thomas Wainewright, 'Pen, Pencil and Poison', published in the *Fortnightly Review* in 1889, Wilde draws Wainewright as himself: 'Of an extremely artistic temperament, [he] followed many masters other than art, being not merely a poet and a painter, an art-critic, an antiquarian, and a writer of prose, an amateur of beautiful things, and a dilettante of things delightful, but also a forger of no mean and ordinary capabilities ...' He says of Wainewright that 'His crimes seem to have had an important effect upon his art. They gave a strong personality to his style, a quality that his early work certainly lacked.' And he concludes that 'there is no essential incongruity between crime and culture.'

Even when he arrived in the Wild West, Wilde had as the principle purpose of his American tour the idea of getting a production of his first play *Vera. Vera*, whose heroine is a Russian nihilist intent on assassinating the Tsar, is just as awe-struck by the glamour of guns as is any mythic penny chapbook account of the deeds of Jesse James. In it, Wilde's attraction to the outlaw life, even to the lone act of violence, is clear. If he is trying to make America more refined in his lectures, the play which he wants to stage there has no such intentions.

Wilde's visit to Lincoln prison took place just nine months after another strange parable of Ireland and America, of fame and infamy, had played itself out there. A young Irish kid, born 21 years earlier in a tenement in New York to a woman, Catherine McCarty, who had fled the Famine in Ireland, was gunned down by a sheriff named Pat Garrett. By the time Wilde arrived in Lincoln, no fewer than five biographies of the young man, Henry McCarty, better known as Billy the Kid, had appeared. They included such titles as *The Cowboy's Career or The Daredevil Career of Billy the Kid, the noted New Mexico Desperado; Billy the Kid and his Girl* ; and Pat Garrett's own account *The Authentic Life of Billy the Kid, the noted Desperado of the Southwest, Whose Deeds of Daring and Blood Have Made His Name a Terror in New Mexico, Arizona, and Northern Mexico.* Garrett's book appeared at the time of Jesse James's similar excursion into the new realms of fame and of Oscar Wilde's parade through America declaring his genius and staking his own claim to fame. While Wilde was preaching the interpenetration of art and life, American popular culture, especially on the frontier, was already practising it.

The blurring of the distinction between fame and notoriety which is so much a part of the afterlife of Jesse James and Billy the Kid, and which would become so much a part of the life of Oscar Wilde, also explodes the distinction between civilisation and barbarism, and indeed between art and life, which was meant to be central to Wilde's American tour.

Long after his return to London, Wilde himself admitted that he was attracted to the 'barbarism' of the Wild West. He enthusiastically welcomed the arrival of Buffalo Bill's Wild West Show in London in 1887. In a typical reversal of accepted wisdom, and in a direct reflection of his own experiences in America, he noted that 'English people are far more interested in American barbarism than in American civilisation.... The cities of America are inexpressibly tedious. The Bostonians take their learning too sadly; culture with them is an accomplishment rather than an atmosphere; their 'Hub', as they call it, is the paradise of prigs... Better the Far West with its grizzly bears and its untamed cowboys, its free open-air life and its free open-air manners, its boundless prairie and its boundless mendacity! That is what Buffalo Bill is going to bring to London; and we have no doubt that London will fully appreciate his show.' As always, when a journalist says 'people', he means 'I'. American barbarism was indeed of far more use to Wilde than American civilisation could ever be.

And indeed, Wilde himself enacted this growing identification with the heroes of the Wild West on his American tour through the most obvious of outward signs — dress. He appeared at first as dandy and aesthete, in long green coat trimmed with seal or otter, turban-like hat, Lord Byron collar and sky-blue tie. But as he progressed through the frontier, he adopted more and more the style of the cowboy and the miner: corduroys and wide-brimmed hat at first, then adding a cowboy neckerchief and tucking his trousers into his boots. Not only did he tell the silver miners of Colorado that they were the best-dressed men in America, but back home in London he preached what they practised. Having himself shocked his American audiences by wearing his own theatrical knee-breeches, he ended up, after his Wild West tour, writing to the editor of the *Pall Mall Gazette* in 1884 to recommend broad-brimmed hats, short cloaks, leather boots, and 'short loose trousers' which are 'in every way to be preferred to the tight knee-breeches which often impede the proper circulation of the blood'.

Wilde, in effect tried to do what Levi Strauss managed to do in the latter half of the twentieth century — to make the working clothes of the American West into a universal consumer fashion for city sophisticates. Contemporary advertisements for Levis and Wranglers, with their fetishisation of cattle-wranglers and manual workers, are following where Wilde led. Tom Wolfe noted in the 1970s that the dress of the wealthy American young now consisted of 'long-distance trucker warms, sheepherder's coats, fisherman's slickers, down-home tenant-farmer bib overalls, coal-stoker strap undershirts, fringed cowpoke jerkins, strike-hall blue workshirts, lumberjack plaids, forest ranger mackinaws, Australian bushrider mackintoshes, Cong sandles, bike leathers, more jeans, jeans, jeans, jeans, jeans, more prole gear of every description than you ever saw or read of in a hundred novels by Jack London, Jack Conroy, Maxim Gorky, Clara Weatherwax and any who came before or after... so that somehow the sons of the slums have become the Brummels and Gentlemen of Leisure, the true fashion plates of 1973...' The proletarian dandy, spawn of Oscar Wilde's encounters with the Wild West, remains a central figure of contemporary consumer culture. If, as Susan Sontag has suggested, modern camp is 'dandyism in the age of mass culture', Wilde's encounter with the obsequies of Jesse James may well be its point of origin.

◆ ◆ ◆ ◆ ◆

Carson: Did you know that one, Parker, was a gentleman's valet, and the other a groom?

Wilde: I did not know it, but if I had I should not have cared. I didn't care twopence what they were. I liked them. I have a passion to civilise the community.

The great American myth, of course, is the myth of the taming of the wilderness, the conquering of the uncivilised Indian by the civilised white man. The Irish played more than their fair part in this process. But that role remains crucially ambivalent. The ambivalence comes from the fact that the Irish are not, in this dichotomy, either/or, they are both/and. They are natives and conquerors, aboriginals and civilisers, a savage tribe in one context, a superior race in another.

Wilde went to America as an Englishman. The letters sent by D'Oyly Carte, who organised the tour, to booking agents, described Wilde as 'the new English poet'. Wilde's original lecture for the tour was on *The English Renaissance*. But the attacks on Wilde by the East Coast establishment take a form that is only possible on the assumption that he is not an Englishman but an Irishman. For what the most serious of those attacks do is to make Wilde a native, a savage, a black man.

The most remarkable of the attacks is a cartoon published on the front page of *The Washington Post* on January 22nd 1882, shortly after Wilde's arrival in America. Titled 'Mr Wild of Borneo', it shows an ape-like humanoid creature holding a coconut in its left hand, and below it, Wilde holding a sunflower in his left hand. The text reads 'How far is it from this (the ape-man) to this (Wilde)?' The caption notes the 'citizen of Borneo, who, so far as we have any record of him, is also Wild, and judging from the resemblance in feature, pose and occupation, undoubtedly akin.'

The second attack in which Wilde is explicitly depicted as a black man came at one of his lectures in Rochester a fortnight later. Half way through the lecture, as arranged by some of the students there, an old black man 'in formal dress and one white kid glove to parody Wilde's attire, danced down the centre aisle carrying an immense bunch of flowers and sat in a front seat.'

These identifications of Wilde with blacks are in fact repeated in England at the height of Wilde's success. In April, 1893, *Punch,* reviewing the opening of *A Woman of No Importance,* referred to its 'Christy Minstrel epigrammatic dialogue' and carried a cartoon called 'Christy Minstrels of No Importance', at the centre of which sits Wilde with the caption 'Massa Johnson O'Wilde'.

These jokes depend on a set of connections between Irish ambivalence (civilised or barbarian?) and theatricality which also work themselves out in the legends of Jesse James and Billy the Kid. However much he wanted to present himself as a civilised Englishman, Wilde was vulnerable to being read as a simian Irishman. And the Irish, in American theatre, were close to the blacks. In popular plays like James Pilgrim's *Katty O'Shea* (1854), the Irish are 'coloured people', unsuitable for marriage to authentic whites. In James Macready's *The Irishman in London* (1853), Murtoch Delaney falls hopelessly in love with his perfect match, the humanoid 'grinning Cuba'.

By insisting on wearing knee-breeches in the early part of his tour, Wilde, perhaps inadvertently, identified himself with the stage Irishman, who was always dressed in them. But the caricatures go far beyond such a casual identification, and *The Washington Post* cartoon in particular draws most explicitly on the nineteenth century image of the Irishman as ape. Its politics and that of *Punch's* strange identification of Wilde with blacked-up minstrels, are made explicit in *Punch's* version of

Darwinism : ' A creature manifestly between the Gorilla and the Negro is to be met with in some of the lowest districts of London and Liverpool by adventurous explorers. It comes from Ireland, whence it has contrived to migrate; it belongs, in fact, to a tribe of Irish savages; the lowest species of the Irish Yahoo.'

Wilde, after his fall, was transformed into an ape-man, 'exhibited like an ape in a cage', the caricature becoming reality, life, in its blackest joke, imitating art.

Being Irish meant that Wilde could never civilise America. His own persona was always open to being annexed to powerful racial images of barbarism, and therefore could never be a stable image of European cultivation. But the Irish ambivalence which made him ultimately incredible as an icon of English civility also allowed him to appropriate American barbarism in the forms which would prove, in the late 20th century, to be most durable as aspects of mass consumer culture. He learned to make a virtue of ambivalence, to combine fame and infamy, proletarian egalitarianism and aesthetic dandyism. He learned how to be criminal and saint, artist and outlaw. He learned how to have it every way. And even though his career took on the logic of his identification with outlaws, the connections which he made between European style and the American frontier remain central to the mass culture of the late twentieth century.

Thirteen years after the auction of the household effects of Jesse James came the auction of the household effects of Oscar Wilde. A hundred years after that came the apotheosis of Oscar Wilde, when his name was inscribed inside Westminster Abbey. In the meantime, the distance between the two men as images of modern fame has, like the distance between civilisation and barbarism, narrowed almost to nothing.

THE WAY WE WERE

Our Boys

Two boys are standing at a bus-stop. They wear the same school uniform, they are the same height, but they do not stand the same way. One has his hands in his pockets, his shoulder propped against the pole, his body slouched like a flag on an airless day. His hair is as tossed as a night on the Atlantic in a force 10 gale, and his school cap is perched on top of it like a small craft about to go under. His school tie dangles from his grubby neck like a miscreant left hanging on the gibbet as a warning to others. His schoolbag, feral and untamed, crouches at his feet, ready to attack passing old ladies or members of the clergy.

The other boy's left arm is straight down by his side, his right tucking his schoolbag snugly into his chaste body. He stands as straight as an exclamation mark and what he exclaims is the honour of his school, his family, his country and the Christian Brothers. His cap sits on his head with the obedience and poise of a well-trained lapdog. His clothes are as unruffled as his smoothly boyish face, whose lustre of serene self-satisfaction sets up a pleasing symmetry with the shine on his shoes. His tie is as straight as a plumbline, pointing to the centre of his moral gravity — his unbreakable, unquestioning faith. He is a good boy. He is the boy I wanted to be.

I remember these drawings from *Courtesy for Boys and Girls*, written and published by the Christian Brothers and used as the basis for a class called Civics, more clearly than anything from any other book I read in childhood. Civics, in theory, was about society and how it worked and, in practice, about good behaviour. You understood, implicitly, that the two things were one and the same, that a society full of good boys standing up straight at the bus-stop would be a good society, that this drawing was a sort of political vision, a large-scale map of Utopia. Me and my friends, the children of housing estates that had not been imagined in the days of national struggle, were the first boy. Through work and prayer and hard discipline, we might become the second.

✦ ✦ ✦ ✦ ✦

Why is man like a tack? I read the riddle in *Our Boys* in 1968, when I was ten years old. Under duress, for we would rather have spent what little money we had on English comics like *The Beano* or *The Dandy* or on American superheroes like *The X-Men*, we bought *Our Boys* at school for sixpence a month. It was a tradition. It had been going since 1914, when it was established by the Christian Brothers with the stated objectives 'to interest, instruct and inspire the boys of our Catholic schools, to create in them a taste for clean literature, to continue the character-forming lessons of their school days, to fire their enthusiasm for what is noble and good, to inflame their love of country, and to help in preserving them as devoted children of Our Holy Mother the Church.' Its masthead carried, under the title, the words 'To God and Eire True' and 'Purity in Our Hearts, Truth on Our Lips, Strength in Our Arms.'

For many years, it was edited by Brother Canice Craven, who had inspired Patrick Pearse and who was famous for having beaten off with his umbrella an assault by a drunken British soldier. He was sent blackthorn sticks by his admirers and his greatest reproof to an obstreperous pupil was that such a naughty boy 'would never die for Ireland'. Brother Canice liked to publish stories about English Protestants persecuting Irish Catholics: 'No mercy for the Papist dogs! Ho, ho!, you rotten Papist!' Not to buy *Our Boys* was to side with those who kicked Papist dogs, to be the boy slouched against the bus-stop, a disgrace not just to your school, but to your country.

I wanted to be a good boy so I coughed up my sixpence and pondered the similarities between man and a tack: 'Man is like a tack because he must be pointed in the right direction, driven hard, and then he will go as far as his head will let him.' This piece of wisdom might well have replaced the more highfalutin' *Facere et Docere* (To Do and To Teach) as the motto of the Christian Brothers. It summed up more precisely what they stood for: the right direction, hard driving, going far. Or, translated into Irish, Catholic faith, strict discipline, social mobility. Out of these three things they made not just an educational system, but an Ireland. They shaped, not just a notion of a country, but many of the conditions in which that country came into existence.

Another riddle: who made the world? As every catechism told us, God made the world. But there were times when it seemed that the Christian Brothers had been his main subcontractors. On the back of all my brick-coloured and red-margined copybooks, full of compound interest, irregular verbs and days at the seaside, was a map of the world. At the centre of this world was Ireland, and arcing out of Ireland like shooting stars were lines leading to Australia, North America, Argentina, Africa — the contours of a spiritual conquest that had begun in 1802 when Edmund Ignatius Rice founded the Christian Brothers in Waterford. Shining over it all was the five-pointed radiant star of the Brothers' logo. It was our Empire, our answer to the British maps of the world in which its colonial possessions glowed scarlet in every continent, while the rest skulked in dull and watery hues. Even when I scratched NFFC (for Nottingham Forest Football Club) into the redbrick paper with the sharp end of my compass, I knew it was their world I was defacing. They had given us our map of the world by giving us our map of Ireland.

'Ireland', said Eamon de Valera in 1944, 'owes more than it will probably ever realise to the Christian Brothers. I am an individual who owes practically everything to the Christian Brothers.' In his memoirs, Todd Andrews, a figure almost as important as de Valera in the creation of independent Ireland, explained why the State owed so much to the heirs of Edmund Rice: 'Without the groundwork of the Christian Brothers' schooling, it is improbable that there would have been a 1916 Rising, and certain that the subsequent fight for Independence would not have been successfully carried through. The leadership of the IRA came largely from those who got their education from the Brothers, and got it free.'

If this claim seems far-fetched, the figures largely bear it out. The extent to which, in the Easter Rising, Christian Brothers boys elbowed aside the Jesuit boys who had imagined themselves as a ruling class in waiting, can be gauged by comparing two schools on the northside of Dublin. The Jesuit Belvedere College supplied five ex-pupils to the ranks of the rebels; the Christian Brothers O'Connell Schools supplied 125. Seven of the 14 men executed as leaders of the Rising were Christian Brothers boys. Three of the five members of the IRA executive elected in 1917, including the chief of staff Cathal Brugha, were in the same category. Of the seven-man Cabinet appointed by the Dail in 1921, five — Kevin O'Higgins, Austin Stack and Arthur Griffith as well as de Valera and Brugha — had spent their schooldays praying for the beatification of Edmund Rice.

Throughout the years in which an independent Ireland was formed, other CBS boys were to the forefront: Terence MacSwiney, Tomas MacCurtain, Liam Lynch, Liam Mellowes, Ernie O'Malley, Sean Treacy, Gerry Boland, Sean Lemass. The impact of the Christian Brothers' schools in forming the minds that formed the State can hardly be overstated. It was not just that the Brothers in what they taught and in the way they taught it, explicitly imparted the message to their pupils that 'Ireland looks to them, when grown to man's estate, to act the part of true men in furthering the sacred cause of nationhood.' It was not just that the Brothers invented and gave currency to the narrative of 800 years of oppression. ('In the martyrology of history, among crucified nations', said the Brothers' *Catechism of Irish History*, 'Ireland occupies the foremost place. The duration of her torture, and the ferocity of her executioner are as revolting as the power of the victim is astonishing.') It was also, more subtly but no less importantly, that they created a generation of educated young men for whom there was no place in British Ireland.

'In a colonial situation', writes the Christian Brother and historian Barry Cowdrey in his book *Faith and Fatherland.*, 'education is inherently revolutionary.' By giving secondary education to lower middle-class youths from Catholic Ireland who then had little prospect of social advancement, the Brothers shaped the discontented young men who shaped the revolution. 'For 35 years before 1916', writes Cowdrey, 'the exceptional achievements of the Brothers' schools in the Intermediate examinations had been creating a pool of well-educated lower middle-class young men who had little to gain from the existing social order and much to hope for in its passing. Educational achievement had raised their economic and social achievements and enhanced their self-respect. It had created the ideal revolutionary group.'

Social mobility and nationalism went hand in hand and the Brothers dealt in both currencies. Having moulded young men who were fit and eager for power, it was almost as if a place in which that power could be taken had to be invented. That place was an independent but implicitly Catholic Ireland. Take up any Christian Brothers' school yearbook from the decades after Independence and you can almost touch the sense of triumph, the naked delight that Our Boys are taking over the State that *Our Boys* has made for them. The Synge Street yearbook for 1946-1947, for instance, opens with a message from an old boy, now a TD and Lord Mayor of Dublin, praising the 'good Brothers who taught me to love God, His Holy Mother and Ireland.' Our Boys are beginning to make good.

There is a spread on 'Our New Attorney-General', a young man called Cearbhall O Dalaigh, later to become president of Ireland, in which the word 'our' has a special emphasis: 'resurgent Ireland is coming into its own.' There is another on 'men on the Air', with pictures of five Synge Street boys who have become 'announcers' on Radio Eireann, among them one Eamonn Andrews. And the seizure of power is only beginning: 'The boys who did the Leaving Certificate in 1945 have gone down to the sea of their dreams in ships with sails courageously unfurled, which even now point to many and diverse ways dream-charted by their youthful pilots...'

Todd Andrews, the ex-Synge Street, ex-IRA man, then managing director of Bord na Mona, is, in an obituary for the school's recently deceased head-brother, most explicit about what is going on : 'Boys attending Synge Street came from modest homes. They had no influence, no contacts, no background, the auspices were not favourable for their advancement in fields of professional endeavour. Brother Roche foresaw the changing times and the shift of power from the alien to the native... He applied his vitality to equip his pupils to take their part in forming the new regime that was coming and actually came as he left Synge Street.' Contacts, influence, advancement. Yet the idea that Edmund Rice, or the martyrs who died for Ireland, might have intended to signify something more profound than equipping the children of the lower middle-class for the dour competition for cushy jobs in a claustrophobic society could not be banished entirely. There was a gap somewhere, a lacuna which could only widen into a dangerous fissure in the apparently stable surface of the monolith the Brothers had done so much to construct.

✦ ✦ ✦ ✦ ✦

Even in the 1960s and 1970s, when I spent my waking hours in the domain of the Christian Brothers, they still had the power to create a comprehensive world view for their pupils. Their certainties shaped our attitudes, in the way that the laws of physics and chemistry shaped our bodies. One brother, teaching us chemistry, cleared the desks from the middle of the room and lined us up on either side. "Ye are all molecules. Ye boys on the right are molecules of sodium. Ye boys on the left are molecules of chlorine." We shrank into ourselves, divesting ourselves of everything in our make-up except the elements he had enunciated. "When I raise my hand, I am applying the heat. Ye will start to shake and shudder." At his command, a quake ran through us and we started to tremble in unison. "Then ye will begin to bounce off each other, one from either side, until a reaction takes place." We threw ourselves blindly forward, crashing into each other with painless violence, anaesthetized by the knowledge that we were insensate molecules obeying the laws of nature.

Even then, I was dimly aware of the metaphoric significance of what we were doing. We were molecules, they were Bunsen burners. Our given stuff was combined into new compounds of their invention. Our characters were formed according to laws as definite as the laws of chemistry. All things were known, even what your Guardian Angel looked like: "His stature is that of a child about nine years old; his aspect full of sweetness and majesty, his eyes generally turned towards heaven, his brow is always serene..." He was, in other words, the good boy at the bus-stop.

We sensed confusions behind the certainties, but could not know how deep they might go. We could not know that shortly after the Brothers' whole reason for existing was formulated, it was diverted into a larger, more cynical, purpose. The Brothers were founded by Edmund Rice specifically to educate the poor — they existed for the destitute, the great unwashed. This remained a part of their self-image, and therefore of ours. Their missionary self-sacrifice defined our gratitude, our awareness of ourselves as children who had no right to be educated and who would have remained in eternal ignorance but for their beneficence.

But the self-image was an illusion. The Brothers may have been founded to teach those who would not otherwise have received an education, but they quickly became an instrument of the Catholic Church's desire to wrest pupils away from the non-sectarian, government-supported National Schools, and to bring them under the control of the Church. "The Brothers' schools", writes Barry Cowdrey, "came to be perceived by Catholic leaders as key factors in their struggle with the government for the control of education in Ireland." The process culminated in 1869 with an explicit threat from Cardinal Cullen, the creator of the modern Irish church, to deny the sacraments to parents who kept their children "in the lion's den" of the National Schools rather than sending them to the Brothers. A principal part of that strategy was that the CBS schools should cater not for the destitute but for the "sons of the better class of the Roman Catholic population". So successful was the campaign to attract the children of comfortable Catholics, and so far had the Brothers strayed from their avowed mission, that by the end of the nineteenth century Archbishop Walsh was referring to a Christian Brothers school in Dublin "from which the poor are virtually excluded".

This contradiction between what the Brothers thought they were and what they actually were was deeply damaging to an institution intimately involved with the mechanics of social mobility. For it created another, deeper, contradiction — between the idea of social mobility that was so much a part of the Brothers' nationalism on the one hand, and the middle-class aspiration to a kind of gentility that was inextricable from the British class system on the other. Apart from Our Boys taking over the new regime, what might social mobility mean? What did it mean to have arrived, and how did a successful *arriviste* behave?

Long after the new State was established, the Brothers were still publishing manuals on etiquette like *Courtesy for Boys and Girls* for use in their own schools and those of the equivalent orders of nuns. Even in Independent Ireland, those manuals assumed that the height of social success would be meeting the British royal family: 'Titles are not frequently repeated in conversation. They hamper too much the freedom of speech which is so necessary to a pleasing intercourse. It is difficult to speak with ease to him who stands on a more elevated plane. Even the Prince of Wales is only addressed 'Sir' in private, and the Queen 'Ma'am'. It is proper, however, with Royalty, to use such an expression as 'Your Royal Highness has just been observing...' These hints on proper behaviour come from an etiquette book, *Christian Politeness and Counsels for Youth*, written by the Christian Brothers and published in Dublin in 1934, two years after Eamon de Valera, who owed everything to them, became Taoiseach for the first time.

The book is riven with a fatal ambivalence. On the one hand, its operative assumption is that its readers have no idea how to behave, that they come from a class and a culture which has never been wealthy enough or stable enough to develop a code of manners. They have learned nothing from their parents, so everything has to be taught — how to walk ('raise the instep a little; this has the effect of stiffening the knee, and placing the shoulders in a graceful position. The step should not be too long, nor yet affectedly short.'), how to sit ('steadily in a rather upright position, with the knees neither too close nor too far asunder, and the feet neither stretched out, nor drawn in so close under the chair as to cause the knees to project.'), what to do with your mouth ('An open mouth denotes feebleness of character. In laughing, we should not expose the gums or make violent contortions of the face.'), where to turn your eyes ('In conversing with superiors it is not well to fix the eyes directly on theirs, but somewhat lower.')

This world is haunted by an inexplicit but inescapable presence — the bad boy at the bus-stop. He is terrifyingly unpredictable, capable at any moment of unimaginable vulgarities. He is one of those young persons who, 'when walking abroad, laugh loudly and in the faces of those they meet'. He picks his teeth 'with a pin or pen-knife'. He has been known to 'spit on the floor, or into the fire, or even on the footways in the streets.' He is apt to drink from his saucer. He 'looks curiously at the plates of others, or scrutinises others while they eat.' He has been known to 'enjoy a man's hospitality and afterwards to abuse his friendship or his confidence.' He can be seen resting his head 'against the wallpaper thereby staining it.' He is 'enraptured with the sight of a highly-coloured picture, while a person of taste, to whom its innumerable defects are visible, can hardly endure to look at it.' He is, in other words, our father or our grandfather, the Irish peasant, the Papist dog.

And yet these Yahoos may, at any moment, find themselves in the presence of Royalty. They need to be armed with the knowledge that 'the title of Honourable is given to the younger sons of Earls, and all the sons and daughters of Viscounts and Barons. Also to the Puisne Judges, and the Barons of the Exchequer, Commissioners of Government Boards, and even the Directors of the Bank of England, East India Company etc, are often styled 'Honourable', but it is only by inferior persons.' He needs to be sure that his calling card is 'of correct size and shape, and... of the best quality of paper.' He must remember that 'he should not, during dinner, reprehend any of the servants for a mistake'. He should be aware of the fact that 'bananas are peeled with the knife and fork, and taken with the fork.' He must recall that 'should tea be served during a morning call, it is usual for gentlemen to remove their gloves.'

In this world-view, just two states of being can be imagined — the bad boy and the good boy at the bus-stop, the ignorant peasant picking his teeth with a pen-knife and the gentleman peeling a banana with a knife and fork, the poor, uncouth Catholic, and the utopian Catholic of the future who had become, in all but religion, a Protestant. The purpose of the Brothers was to provide a passage from one state to the other. Their problem was that they could not imagine anything outside the inherited categories of stage Irishman and stage Englishman. They were locked in the colonial antithesis of wild natives and civilised denizens of the mother country, an antithesis they had merely internalised, imagining themselves as missionaries from a mother country that was also mother church. They could not allow for the possibility of profound change in the way people might behave or in the make-up of social hierarchies. They could not envisage the way a society like the one that was being formed in my childhood — shaped above all by the demotics of American popular culture — might work.

Nor could they imagine the Ireland that they themselves had done so much to create and that I was living in. They had no hold on urban life, on television, or on rock music, no way of coping with the forces that were seeping ineluctably into our souls. Indeed, they could not even cope with Independent Ireland. Instead of trying to come up with some Catholic X-Men, the *Our Boys* that I was reading in the late 1960s and early 1970s, was still full of second-hand versions of English *Boy's Own* stories of the 1920s, sometimes with Irish names superimposed on the characters, sometimes not. The schools in the stories were English public schools where boys strolled across the quad and had fights with fellows called 'Greene of Middle School', uttering expletives like 'great pip!', giving 'a first class ribbing' to this 'chump' or that 'rotter'. At best, the boy delivering the ribbing was called Murphy instead of Bunter or Brown.

In the adventure stories, Irish names were freely scattered: 'Corporal Sean Dowling of the Canadian Mounted Police sighed contentedly' or 'The Lazy L ranch was shorthanded just now and O'Leary would be very glad to have the active young Irishman on his payroll...' But just as often, no attempt was made to evade the irony that in 1960s Ireland, 50 years after the Easter Rising, the Brothers were still peddling stories about firm-jawed Englishmen facing up to shifty Arabs or squaring off against the mysterious natives of darkest Africa: 'And many a time had Derek heard the tale of how his uncle stole the amulet from the arm of the Great One, Amen-Atop, in that temple half-buried by the sand, away out in the desert beyond Cairo. His uncle Jack, then a youngster in the Fifth Northshires — part of the force stationed in Egypt in those far-off days before people like Nasser were ever heard of — had all the average youngster's hairbrained passion for adventure, and the more risky the better.'

The only version of Ireland, the only language which was not imbued with rotters and boys called Kennedy Minor, was that of the Kitty the Hare stories, full of thatched cottage verities. To me it was literally incomprehensible: 'Musha, I'm thinking, that he'd just as soon not have his brother Jeremiah coming to the house at all at all. You see, Jeremiah never pulled well with Paddy, Kitty, and as Father Malachy told us, when he got the letter from Boston, Jeremiah is just as hard on poor Paddy as ever he was. God help us! So 'tis no wonder Paddy wouldn't be very eager to see Jeremiah again!' It was a language even more foreign than 'great pip!' and 'rotter', which were at least more familiar from the books I was reading — Biggles, Enid Blyton, Billy Bunter. Between that improbable England and that impossible Ireland, the country I was actually living in got lost.

While the students of Paris were on the barricades, and my father and the other busmen of Dublin were on strike,

I was reading in *Our Boys* about Maurice, who got a nice girl, joined the Saint Vincent de Paul Society, and became a good boy: 'He was getting on better with his boss. Before, he had always been pushing for more pay, or looking for easier work, or something. But now he didn't mind getting the toughest job — and the dirtiest — and he was always willing to change his shift to suit someone else.'

While the world was mourning the death of Martin Luther King, I was reading the Murphy story *Murphy and the Boy from Africa*:

'"Meet Zaka the Zulu', grinned Curtis. 'Exa balla murullo!', said Zaka, or words to that effect, bowing low instead of taking the proferred hand. 'Eh?' 'Samaruddy jara waramacky!', said the boy from Africa amiably. 'A nigger from Africa is expected at St Michaels', said Murphy, his eyes gleaming. 'All right, a nigger will turn up, only it won't be the genuine article. It'll be little me."'

❖ ❖ ❖ ❖ ❖

In the gap between the reality and the image, there was a fearful darkness. The only aspect of the *Our Boys* stories that made real sense to me was the constant violence of boys being "spiflicated": 'Yarooh!', howled Murphy. Whack! 'Yow-ow-ow!' Each whack wrung an anguished yell from Murphy and there were smothered chuckles from the black-robed figures standing around.' Cries of pain and black-robed figures belonged together. Violence and inchoate sexuality were the expressions of troubled confusion on the part of the Brothers — not because they had any monopoly on these things in a society where violence against children and sexual repression were the norm, but because they were themselves haunted by their failure to control them. Corporal punishment was so inescapable a part of a Christian Brothers education (practised at least as much by the lay teachers as by the Brothers themselves), that we never suspected that there might be inner turmoil within the order itself with feelings of shame and revulsion finding at least intermittent expression.

As far back as 1861, the Brothers were racked by the fear that their teaching methods might be at odds with their mission. In that year, the Superior General Brother Michael Riordan, sent a circular to all his members, bemoaning the fact that Brothers who were not able to win the trust of their pupils by force of personality were resorting to "the humiliating alternative of enforcing submission by coercive measures": "The subject being of too painful a nature for lengthened detail, we prefer to throw a veil over its naked deformity; but nevertheless we cannot omit strongly exhorting you to exhibit and practice towards these poor children that paternal tenderness and solicitude peculiar to God's chosen servants."

For much of the order's history, that veil over the naked deformity of violence remained securely in place. But in private at least the doubts remained. In 1930, the Superior General Brother J.P. Noonan decided that corporal punishment had to be entirely outlawed: "Abuses have arisen; and they will recur, I fear, as long as our regulations give any authority for the infliction of corporal punishment. Let us aim at its complete abolition in our schools, and anticipate legislation which would make its infliction illegal." Yet, for nearly half a century after, the Brothers continued with abuses which their own Superior had believed should not only be discouraged but made illegal.

Sexual unease was even more difficult to articulate. In 1920, the Superior Brother Patrick Hennessy listed "the fondling of boys" almost casually among the inconsequential bad habits he wanted to stamp out. "How many are the temptations from which a modest guard of the eyes will save us as we walk through the streets of a town or city! I have sometimes seen Religious peering into tramcars as they sped by and surely not to the edification of the passengers... The fondling of boys, the laying of hands upon them, in any way, is contrary to the rules of modesty, and is decidedly dangerous. I have sometimes seen Brothers in the playgrounds of the schools with their hands in their habit pockets — this is an ungraceful pose. I have sometimes seen brothers who discarded the biretta for a felt or other hat, and some who discarded the cincture. Such things should not occur."

Later, the tone in which such things were discussed within the order became more anguished. An internal guidebook for Brothers, *The Soul of Our Vocation,* used by them in the 1960s and 1970s, deals uneasily with the separation from family life and sexual relationships that was part of their lot: "The revolt of our senses, which is an unavoidable consequence of our nature... is very strong since the fall of our first parents, and we may all have to feel the demands of the sensible parts of our nature against the restraint of right reason. It is important that there should be no surprise when this happens to us, and certainly there should be no panic."

The author goes on to quote from Saint Paul and his dramatisation of the war between the rational mind and the genitals: "For I know that in me (that is, in my flesh) dwelleth no good thing... but how to perform that which is good I find not. For the good that I would I do not; but the evil which I would not, that I do... For I delight in the law of God after the inward man but I see another law in my members, warring against the law of my mind, and bringing me into captivity to the law of sin which is in my members."

In such a struggle, rules have to be formulated which are the result "of experience, and in many cases sad experience". The author admonishes his fellow-Brothers that "while avoiding the extreme hardness of heart and a puritanical outlook, there must be no emotionalism, and all excessively sentimental friendships must be avoided, particularly with the young who are placed in our charge and with whom we are so often in contact... The contacts we have to make with the boys of our schools must be spiritualised, and we must avoid entirely a too natural friendship which would only be the expression of the instinct of fatherhood inherent in us all. Similarly, social engagements and visiting seculars is generally an indication of our natural attraction to the home life of a family. As individuals, we should allow ourselves to be forgotten when we have done our duty to the best of our ability."

Such restraints, the author accepts, will lead to inevitable scandals: "It must needs be scandals come (Matthew, 18.7) Let not such discourage us or induce us to follow a lax example, because the failure of some should only be an incentive to greater loyalty on the part of others."

Behind this strained, painfully evasive language, lay the reality of the scandals that needs must come, and that, in the early 1990s, began to emerge.

❖ ❖ ❖ ❖ ❖

And so, even at the height of their power, the Brothers were being destroyed from the inside. What we took to be their certainty was merely the cover for a deep and inarticulate turmoil. When change came, the certainties, eaten away from the inside, crumbled, and the institution which had been one of the apparently immutable bastions of Irish society, collapsed within an astonishingly short period. The social mobility which the Brothers had created for the pupils whom James Joyce described in *A Portrait of the Artist as a Young Man* as "Paddy Stink and Mickey Mud" could not be controlled. The boys the Brothers boasted of as evidence of their success — boys like Sean Lemass, Cearbhall O Dalaigh, Eamonn Andrews and Gay Byrne — went on to create another Ireland, profoundly different from the one that the Brothers had helped to invent. The forces the Brothers had unleashed on British Ireland, the revolutionary discontent they had engendered, were now turned back on themselves.

Three quarters of the remaining Irish Christian Brothers are over 50, and the trickle of new recruits — less than ten a year — will barely be enough to care for the aged ones. Many Brothers left to get married, many of those who remain are dedicated radicals, more interested in turning society upside down than in oiling its wheels. The 'resurgent Ireland coming into its own' is no longer theirs. Some Brothers' schools, like the one I went to, have closed altogether. Others have been handed over to boards of management, and lay principals have been appointed by an order that once urged that lay teachers be "kept in their proper place" and not spoken to by Brothers unless absolutely necessary.

Meanwhile, the bad boy is still slouched against the bus-stop, his school cap blown into the gutter, his hair shaved off or dyed a fetching pink, his hands not merely deep in his pockets but moving about with suspicious fumbles. The other boy, the good one I used to want to be, took the last bus home long ago, and sits in a still, airless room peeling bananas with a knife and fork.

The Irish for
Ho Ho Ho

For a few years now, I have been Santa Claus in the Christmas fete at my sons' school. I approach the job with mixed feelings.

On the one hand, it is chastening to realise that only in a red suit with two pillows shoved up inside the jacket and with most of my face hidden by a itchy white beard can I manage to look benevolent and cheerful instead of cynical and lugubrious. On the other, the experience is strangely and wonderfully touching. It makes you realise that there is still a capacity for wonder in the world.

Santa's grotto is usually in the corner of a familiar classroom, marked off with a makeshift arrangement of black plastic bags, crepe paper and tinsel. Virtual reality it isn't. Entering this somewhat tacky domain to find a stooped and suspiciously thin figure with absurd strands of some synthetic fibre straddling his harrassed-looking face and pathetic wisps of greying hair peeping out from under his hood, any self-repsecting four-year old, steeped in Bart Simpson's streetwise cynicism, ought to raise the alarm.

The astonishing thing is that very few of them do. There is always the odd nine year-old wiseguy, but the pressure of a heavy Santa-type toecap on a Nike-trainered toe usually ensures silence. Mostly, from the younger kids, there is the purest and most naked awe. And, from the older ones there is something more remarkable still — a conscious decision to be fooled. They can see the awkward illusion for what it is, but they actually choose to go along with it, to play out a ritual that, for all its dodgy exterior, still has for them an inner meaning.

The fact is that in an age when few rituals, even very serious ones, can retain their force, Santa Claus still works. And it is not just the story — the cosy narrative of snow-bound toy-factories, elves, reindeer, chimneys and stockings — that works, but also the visual code. Even in the most unpromising of circumstances, with an ageing journalist in a second-hand suit sitting in a corner of a draughty classroom, the suit, the beard, the hood, the boots, the belt, the bulging belly, have an irresistible allure.

And the interesting thing is that this visual code is itself neither very old nor very hallowed. It was invented in its finished form — the red suit with white trimmings, the white beard, the twinkly old eyes — in the 1930s by an artist commissioned to create an image of Santa Claus for a Coca Cola advertisement. That image itself drew on the promiscuous range of cultures thrown into the American melting pot: Saint Nicholas from Asia Minor via Holland, Scandinavian pagan legends of Yule Buck, Father Christmas from England.

For cultural purists, Santa was a nightmare, an example of modern inauthenticity at its very worst. Irish cultural nationalists were no exception, and though it is now forgotten, one of their projects was to replace Santa with an authentic Gaelic figure. For Christmas, 1917, the Irish Ireland movement produced T.H. Nally's *Finn Varra Maa — The Irish Santa Claus* at the Theatre Royal. It was, as its title suggested, a conscious attempt to repel the invasion of the alien Santa.

Early in the play, the old granny — there was always an old granny — sings a song which includes the lines:

In England they have one they call 'Father
   Christmas'
A grey-bearded Russian they dub 'Santa Claus',
But here in the fair land of Erin we dismiss
Their Muscovite fairies with white-whiskered jaws.
They've stolen our Poetry, Music, and Stories,

Our orators, statesmen, our letters and art
But they shall not rob us of our ancient glories
They're guarded too well in each true Irish heart.

The production was bedecked with the standard images of Ireland — thatched cottages, spinning wheels, bog-deal dressers, and a wolfhound of whom *The Evening Herald* noted that "The wolfhound squatting on his haunches and occasionally biting himself was nobly Irish..."

Instead of Santa, true Irish children were to expect a visit from Finn Varra Maa. Finn would come down the chimney at midnight and leave toys made by fairies. But he would live the rest of the year, not in the alien North Pole, but in Connemara. He would wear, not a red suit and a fluffy beard, but a fairy cloak and hat. And since there was no mention of reindeer, he would travel, presumably, by ass and cart.

All of this was not entirely laughable. The idea that people should have their own culture, their own images of benevolence and goodwill, was by no means unreasonable. But to judge from contemporary reviews, it may have been somewhat boring. *The Evening Herald* applauded the idea and tried very hard to make it all sound exciting, but wondered in an aside "whether it is not a little too simple for our average Irish theatre-goer, brought up on the 'guffawed' goods imported from across channel." Even 80 years ago, the idea of cultural purity was a bit too simple for most Irish people.

Poor Finn, of course, never caught on, probably because he missed the point — that spirits are meant to be, not familiar and authentically rooted in native soil, but strange and exotic. But probably also because it is exactly the mongrel nature of Santa Claus, his lack of a proper pedigree, that makes him so resonant. He is everything that an enduring icon should not be — synthetic, manufactured, makey-up. But he is a great celebration of accidental cultural collisions, of glorious impurity. He lives in the North Pole because he comes from nowhere, and coming from nowhere can belong everywhere.

The fact is that when it comes to symbols, most of us would prefer Santa's flying reindeer any day to a nobly Irish wolfhound sitting on his haunches and occasionally biting himself. Authentic cultures do tend to end up gnawing on their own tails, turning inwards with puritan disdain on themselves. Images that are obviously invented, on the other hand, are infinitely open. Santa works because people, whatever their cultures, can still make an image their own, can still invest it with personal meanings and emotions, and still have a capacity for hope and wonder that transcends the evidence of their eyes.

Like the children who reckon that Santa doesn't exist, but choose to believe in him anyway, cultures can learn to enjoy operating on more than one level at the same time. They can believe in the authenticity of things even if they are impure. Given the consequences of the pursuit of cultural purity in both parts of Ireland, they know that those who can't manage such an act of faith will wake up to a sack of ashes.

I Gotta Gal in Kalamazoo: The Easy Defeat of Official Ideology

Looking back from the mid-1990s, after the old ideology of conservative Catholic nationalism in the Republic of Ireland has been so sadly reduced, the question that occurs is not why it was so strong but why it was so easily defeated. Because it lingered so long after its social basis had been destroyed, because it had victories on abortion and divorce in the 1980s that turned out to be pyrrhic but looked decisive, it made sense to believe that it was a formidable construct. And yet, with a few huffs and puffs, it fell down.

In the first years of the 1990s, it suddenly collapsed in extraordinary disarray. Ministers belonging to Fianna Fail, the party that had seemed to be one of the western world's great power-holding operations were going on television pleading with the public to believe that, in the events surrounding the collapse of Albert Reynolds's government in late 1994, they were stupid rather than corrupt. Cardinal Daly, the head of the Catholic Church in Ireland was being laughed at and treated with derision on the *Late Late Show* by an audience made up entirely of Catholic priests and nuns.

It is true, of course, that the basis for the old ideology was eroded by fundamental changes in the nature of Irish society. Industrialisation and urbanisation, the spread of education, the effects of television — all made a degree of secularisation and scepticism inevitable. But the real question is why the old ideology was so bad at dealing with those changes. Why was it unable to adapt to urban life, to invent images of modernity that would successfully incorporate the old assumptions? Why, when push came to shove, did it seem so bewildered?

The collapse was, at least at one level, the obverse of the power. It happened in part because, at its height, the official ideology was so strong that it did not seem to need to do what the best ruling classes always do: co-opt the opposition. Through the arrogance of power, it had created a situation in which the treason of the intellectuals was inevitable because the intellectuals had nothing to be loyal *to*. And, at the same time, it had become so dependent on rural romanticism that it had also made images of modern life necessarily images of opposition.

In Denis Johnston's play *The Old Lady Says No!*, written in 1926, the hero, who believes himself to be Robert Emmett, encounters the Irish artistic establishment. There is the 'well-known dramatist' Seamus O'Cooney, a caricature of Sean O'Casey, muttering to himself about the 'maddenin', minglin' memories of the past'. There is O'Mooney, the 'rising portrait painter', and O'Rooney, 'the famous novelist'. And there is the host of the party at which all are gathered, The Minister for Arts and Crafts. 'Talent', the Minister announces, 'is what the country wants. Politics may be all OK in their way, but what I want to say to An Taoiseach is this, that until we have Talent and Art in the country, we have no National Dignity. We must have Talent and Art. Isn't that right?'

The Minister goes on:

'Now see here, I'm Minister for Arts and Crafts, you see. Well, a young fellow comes along to me and he says, Now look, Liam, here's some Art I'm after doing... it might be a book, you see, or a drawing, or even a poem... and can you do anything for me, he says? Well, with that, I do... if he deserves it, mind you, only if he deserves it, under Section

15 of the Deserving Artists (Support) Act, no. 65 of 1926. And there's none of this favouritism at all.

CHORUS: The State supports the Artist.

GRATTAN: And the Artist supports the State.

CHORUS: Very satisfactory for everybody and no favouritism at all.

MINISTER (confidentially): And of course then, you see, it helps us to keep an eye on the sort of stuff that's turned out, you understand.

CHORUS: Clean and pure Art for clean and pure people."

What is striking about this scene, however, is that its satire is almost entirely misplaced. The State had no Minister for Arts and Crafts. (The Second Dail had a Ministry for Fine Arts, which lasted all of 19 weeks.) More importantly, neither the Cosgrave nor the de Valera governments ever had the degree of cultural sophistication necessary for a State to simultaneously seduce and keep an eye on its artists. For a political project that was so intimately bound up from the start with a cultural project, Irish political nationalism in fact proved to be very bad at constructing a broader ideology in which the State would support the artists and the artists would support the State. In this failure, which was critical to the long-term erosion of the nationalist project, the State's broad alliance with religious conservatism got in the way of the alliance it might have made with artists and intellectuals.

Everyone is familiar with the repression of art in the Irish state up to the late 1960s and in particular with the horrors of censorship. But that general picture requires two qualifications. The first is that it is important to understand the censorship as negative rather than positive, as in effect the absence of a viable cultural project on the part of the State rather than an attempt to impose one. Whereas in the Soviet Union, for instance, State censorship was allied to the development of an official art, supported both financially and institutionally by the government, in Ireland censorship was all stick and no carrot. The second qualification is that too little attention has been paid to the role of artists and artistic institutions themselves, even in the absence of censorship by the State, in the repression of cultural vitality. These two qualifications do not absolve the State in de Valera's Ireland from Sean O'Faolain's charge of philistinism, but they do suggest something even more depressing: that even if there had been no censorship, the position of artists and intellectuals would not have been appreciably better.

What is especially notable about the early career of Sean O'Faolain, the chief intellectual dissident in nationalist Ireland indeed, is the way it suggests that literary censorship may have been genuinely detrimental to the interests of the State. Informal censorship by right-wing pressure groups and the fear of institutions like the Abbey that they might offend the government or the audience kept theatre in line. A little more subtlety on the part of the State — the mutual back-scratching advocated by Johnston's Minister for Arts and Crafts — might well have controlled literature in precisely the same way without creating the kind of coherent opposition that O Faolain and Peadar O'Donnell, together with intellectuals like Owen Sheehy-Skeffington and Hubert Butler were able to muster.

With hindsight, it is easy to forget how easily even Sean O'Faolain could have been co-opted by the new State, and indeed how hard he tried to be co-opted. O'Faolain was, of course, a propagandist for the Republican side in the Civil War. Most of his generation of Republicans made their peace with the new State when de Valera split from Sinn Fein, founded Fianna Fail and took power through the ballot box in 1932. Since O'Faolain was himself disillusioned with the militaristic nationalism of the rump Sinn Fein, he could easily have been a part of this final settling of accounts.

That he was not was largely the fault of the new establishment. He wrote a sycophantic biography of de Valera that he himself afterwards characterised as 'shamelessly pro-Dev and pro-Irish propaganda.' And he canvassed for the job of Professor of English at University College Cork, a job that, had he got it, would have made him a semi-official cultural ideologue of the new State. He tried to make himself acceptable to the governors of the university, including the Bishop of Cork and the farmer he canvassed in his field whose only question was 'A professor of English? Can you talk Irish?'

He was, nevertheless, overwhelmingly defeated for the job by Daniel Corkery, who had the same Republican credentials but a much more potent neo-Wagnerian ideology of race and nationality, one that held that only writers whose work was dominated by Catholicism, Irish nationalism and the Land, could be regarded as properly Irish at all. To that defeat was added the insult of censorship. When his rather innocuous book of stories *Midsummer Night Madness* was banned in Ireland in 1932, he was being pushed into exile, either internal or external. Through the stupidity of censorship, Fianna Fail lost the possibility of an alliance with an intellectual whose political background and personal ambitions could, in other circumstances, have inclined him to do the State some service.

But many artists also colluded in this process. The fate of *The Old Lady Says No!* itself is instructive in this regard. When Johnston discussed the play with Lady Gregory, who rejected it, giving it its title in the process, she told him that 'We liked the little play it starts with very much, but later on we thought it got a bit common.' The little play with which it starts is a deliberately ludicrous pastiche of Irish nationalist romanticism, sewn together from lines of Thomas Moore, Aubrey de Vere and James Clarence Mangan. It is clean and pure Art for clean and pure people. But it seemed to fit within an acceptable ideological frame. Had Johnston been prepared to make an entire play from these ironic shavings from the worm-ridden writing-desk of Irish Romanticism, Lady Gregory at least would probably have been happy to produce the play.

W. B. Yeats, to his credit, was more pragmatic and clear-headed, if not more admirable, in his reasons for refusing the play. According to Johnston, Yeats told him 'If we put on your play, we will alienate our audience and lose £50. We don't mind losing the £50, but we don't want to alienate our audience.' And the combination of Lady Gregory's and Yeats's reasons for rejecting the play is indicative of the forces that made de Valera's Ireland a cultural desert. Instead of actually setting about the job of creating a coherent, distinctively Irish, conservative ideology, all the pressure was towards a combination of cynicism and crassness.

For a time, the Free State, when it thought of art at all, seemed likely to develop an attitude remarkably similar to that of Soviet Socialist Realism. Michael Collins expected that native artists would be, in the new Ireland 'more than the mere producers of verse and the painters of pictures. They will teach us, by their vision, the noble race we may become, expressed in their poetry and their pictures. They will inspire us to live as Irish men and women should.' But since what 'we may become' was to be found only in the West, the artists would be expected to look for it there. And since the moral and spiritual role of the artist came within the sphere of the Church, it was fitting that the Catholic Church should become, for the early decades of the new State, by far the largest patron of the arts, commissioning painters and sculptors, shaping public taste, influencing styles and attitudes. But the problem for both Church and State was that neither could manage to encompass ordinary urban life within the developing iconography.

Paul Henry, Sean O'Sullivan, Sean Keating and Maurice MacGonigal were the semi-official painters of the new

State. The *Irish Free State Official Handbook* (1932) features a Paul Henry landscape on its cover and draws heavily on the work of the others inside.

Likewise, the paintings commissioned by the Electricity Supply Board to glorify and record the electrification of the countryside are remarkably Socialist Realist in their heroic posturing and grim formality. Keating's famous image of *The Key Men*, showing dashingly handsome engineers directing the building of a power station is sharply ideological. It follows Michael Collins's call for uplifting visions of the Irish future under construction. The central figure, with his chiselled features, distant gaze and raised arm, his jaunty scarf and quasi-military attire, could be taken from a Soviet image of Lenin or Stalin.

The very title bespeaks a vanguardism that is appropriate to the style. These are the visionaries, the planners, the brains. Behind them, barely visible, are the ant-like workers carrying out their orders. The title also, conveniently, manages to obscure the fact that many of the 'key men' in the early development of the ESB were foreign experts. And this, as well as other ESB paintings by Keating and MacGonigal, also provides a way of depicting workers without having to depict towns or cities. In images like Keating's *No 8 Excavator at Work* and MacGonigal's *The Clady Scheme* the activity of work is largely divorced from the awkward presence of workers and cities. We get landscapes — sky, earth, mountains — and we get machines. The actual workers are small, irrelevant, details.

And these mild allusions to the existence of wage labourers are about as far as it went. Indeed, the obdurate refusal to deal with the actual Ireland in which the artist was living is overpowering. To be an Irish painter was to attach oneself to the search for the 'real' Ireland that lay beyond the fallen, Anglicised world of Dublin and Belfast.

In this respect, Paul Henry is an archetypal figure. A product of urban, evangelical Protestant Belfast, his re-invention of himself as an artist involved a chosen devotion of the West. Significantly, he arrived on Achill Island via Paris and an immersion in the work of Millet. Millet lies behind the monumental, eternal pictures of rural archetypes — fishermen launching a currach, potato diggers, turf cutters — that Henry made. The sense of absence in his work, the disappearance of Belfast, of Protestants, of urban workers, is overwhelming, and, in the end, literal. As his work develops, it becomes more and more clear that the human figures are mere adjuncts to the landscape, devoid of any relationship to the economic world, and eventually the human figure disappears altogether. His subject is narrowed down to sky, sea, mountain and thatched cottages.

It may not be a coincidence that two of the most powerful figures in the official ideological apparatus of the State — Ernest Blythe and Henry — were Ulster Protestants, men whose own culture was deemed by Catholic nationalist ideology not to exist at all. Their sense of Irish 'reality' was one which was shaped by a refusal to deal with their own backgrounds. Having denied themselves, they had no difficulty in denying the other anomalies of Irish life.

Paul Henry's vision of Achill, where he spent the critical years of his artistic development, could almost be a conscious carrying out of a programme laid down by Michael Collins, in an article published in 1922: "In the island of Achill, impoverished as the people are, hard as their lives are, difficult as the struggle for existence is, the outward aspect is a pageant. One may see processions of young women riding down on the island ponies to collect sand from the seashore, or gathering in the turf, dressed in the shawls and in their brilliantly-coloured skirts... They remain simple and picturesque. It is only in such places that one gets a glimpse of what Ireland may become again."

On the other hand, Collins's article could almost be a political programme inspired by Henry's paintings. The politics of 'what Ireland may become' are saturated in visual imagery of 'outward aspect', of pageant, of brilliant colours. Both the paintings and the politics are the result of willed absences, of a conscious turning away from a culture that is urban and industrial.

When, in 1941, Paul Henry had to produce a picture of Belfast to go with a guide book written by Sean O'Faolain, the image is as distant as possible and conforms as closely as possible to his Western landscapes. The picture is called *Belfast from Greencastle*, so that the perspective is literally that from a fishing village across the Lough from the city, ensuring that the point-of-view is on acceptable, non-urban ground. The top three quarters of the painting is sky, like any Western sky. Almost the entire bottom quarter is sand and sea. Between these safe blocks of landscape runs a thin thread of urban skyline, shadowy steeples and murky chimneys belching out foul smoke that threatens to obliterate the beauties of nature. That is all that this Belfastman can see of his native city.

It is not accidental that many of the images of workers and cities painted in the South are the work of women, who were largely outside of the official ideological construct. Urban life was left to women artists because both artist and subject were seen as being minor. Yet, paradoxically, this very assumption allowed women painters to appropriate large areas of politics and economics. They were able, not merely to portray workers, but to subvert the accepted images of labour as male and industrial.

This process reached its zenith in the commissioning of Gabriel Hayes to do the carvings for the Department of Industry and Commerce building in Kildare Street in Dublin. She was not among the five artists originally asked to submit designs, and only got on the shortlist when one of them, Oliver Sheppard, died. Yet her images are among the very few monuments to labour in Ireland. Abstract and impersonal, they nevertheless celebrate labour itself with a rare inclusiveness and breadth. Her designs incorporate craft workers and factory workers, men and women, and reflect the brief shift towards an ideology of dynamic development that followed Fianna Fail's coming to power in the 1930s, and the attempt to shift the Department of Industry and Commerce away from what Todd Andrews described as its belief that 'the efficient pastoralisation of the country would be enough to produce national prosperity'. Yet that period of Fianna Fail radicalism was brief, and it did not have enough ideological steam behind it to allow for the emergence of a new official iconography in which workers and industry could replace peasants and land. Gabriel Hayes's designs stand out as the exceptions that prove the rule, traces of what the official ideology might have achieved — included urban and industrial life within its scope — but didn't.

The problem, in a sense was that the maintenance of the official ideology was too easy. It could be managed even without direct and heavy-handed State interference. The place of theatre in de Valera's Ireland is especially instructive because, unlike cinema and literature, theatre was not subjected to formal censorship. Yet even in the absence of legal controls, conformity could be maintained by a mixture of fear of losing state subsidy, of right-wing Catholic agitation in the theatre itself, and of ideological conformity on the part of the *apparatchiks*. Theatre was easily repressed by a combination of nationalist ideology and philistinism. The rejection by the Abbey of *The Old Lady Says No!* in 1929, together with the contemporaneous rejection of O'Casey's *The Silver Tassie* marks the real cultural beginning of the Irish Free State.

Sean O'Faolain, in one of his early works, the play *She Had to Do Something,* staged at the Abbey in 1937, reflected, as Lennox Robinson had done in *Drama At Inish,* on the effective banishment of theatricality from the public realm. In the play, which is based on incidents that took place when the Anna Pavlova Dance Company visited the Cork Opera House in 1931, a Frenchwoman living in a small Irish town brings in a Russian ballet to liven things up. The ballet horrifies the locals and is driven out. But proving the impossibility of satire in the Ireland of the 1930s, an organised group in the audience at the opening night in the Abbey howled the same protests at the play as the characters had against the ballet. The piece both enacted and provoked the effective banishment of theatre by organised reaction.

A decade earlier, in 1924, Ernest Blythe as Minister for Finance had made the Abbey the first state-sponsored theatre in the English-speaking world, creating the possibility of an alliance between the State and its most important cultural institution that might have harnessed the genuine creative energies of the theatre for an offical ideological project. Instead, the Abbey became, in effect, a withered arm of the State itself, with all the creative energy of a civil service department. The rejection of Johnston and O'Casey, together with the exclusion of another experimentalist in form and content, George Fitzmaurice, created a theatrical art that would not be positive enough to support the State, but that would be so vitiated as to be incapable of threatening it. By 1941, Blythe himself had become managing director of the Abbey, completing a process of bringing Irish theatre under the direct control of conservative politics.

But that control was almost entirely negative. It was exercised essentially by *not* putting on plays, by creating a vacuum filled only by an astonishing mediocrity. Blythe's policy at the Abbey was dominated by his belief that the theatre should be a tool for the revival of the Irish language. But since there was virtually no play writing of any quality in the Irish language, what was actually produced was work that could be unbelievably fatuous. The State ended up undermining its own ideological project — that of producing a distinctive native culture. Blythe's contribution to the Abbey's official history, published just after the fire of 1951, is eloquent in its unsatirisible demonstration of the ludicrous logic of the policy:

"On 26th December 1945, an event took place which was an innovation in the work of the Abbey theatre — Pantomime entirely in the Irish language was performed. Although the Directors would not regard Pantomime in English as being a suitable activity for the Theatre, they considered, having regard to all the facts of Irish life, and to the national policy — enshrined in the Constitution and endorsed by successive Governments — of fostering the Irish language, that the Abbey theatre ought to undertake Pantomime in Irish. The 1945 Pantomime was based on the same folk tale as Lady Gregory used for her *Golden Apple*."

Unfortunately, no text of this masterwork survives, but Peter Kavanagh, who was there, gives us some idea in his book on the Abbey of just what Blythe had made of the tradition of Lady Gregory: 'This performance included a 'leg show' and its highest point of distinction was the excellent translation of the popular hit *I Got a Gal in Kalamazoo*.'

To understand what was lost in the translation from Kiltartan to Kalamazoo, you need some idea of what was displaced by the Gaelic Panto. After the old Abbey was demolished in 1961, its stones and bricks were used to lay a pathway in Deans Grange cemetery. This was an appropriate end for them, for the Abbey in de Valera's time was a graveyard of theatrical invention. The Abbey under Blythe and Radio Eireann offered the two main State-subsidised outlets for would-be Irish playwrights. Yet the list of plays rejected by one or other or by both reads like an order of merit:

Seamus Byrne's *Little City*, about abortion, rejected by the Abbey in 1952, and not staged at all until ten years later. His *Design for a Headstone* banned on Radio Eireann in the mid-1950s even though it was actually in rehearsal. Brendan Behan's *The Quare Fellow* rejected by the Abbey in 1954. John B.Keane's *Sive* rejected by Blythe and Tomas MacAnna at the Abbey and by Radio Eireann in 1959.

Later in the same year, Keane's *Sharon's Grave* was rejected by the Abbey. Blythe apparently found the characters 'too grotesque for words'. According to Keane, though, 'Before I sent the manuscript to the Abbey, I deliberately glued two pages together and when I got it back they were still untouched.' Tom Murphy's *A Whistle in the Dark* turned down by Blythe in 1961 on the basis that the characters were unreal, the atmosphere incredible, and that no such people existed in Ireland.

What all of these plays have in common is that they are either set in cities (two of them, *Design for a Headstone* and *The Quare Fellow* are set in prison) or, as in Keane's case, they give a fierce and bleak view of rural Ireland. The problem for the official ideology was that it had nothing to put in their place. All it could do was to hold on to a version of Ireland that had never been especially convincing, but that, as time went on and the society changed beyond recognition, was becoming blatantly fantastic.

It is hard for instance to comprehend just how pervasive and long-lasting was the ideological insistence on Ireland as an essentially peasant culture. As late as 1961, two years after the First Programme of Economic Expansion, we find the RTE radio drama producer and Abbey director Michael O hAodha writing that 'It is worth noting that the best original Abbey plays of the last 25 years — MacNamara's *Margaret Gillan*, Carroll's *Shadow and Substance*, Teresa Deevy's *Katie Roche*, M.J. Molloy's *King of Friday's Men*, Seamus Byrne's *Design for a Headstone* — are every bit as much peasant plays as *The Fiddler's House* or *In The Shadow of the Glen*. This is understandable in an agricultural country where most town and city dwellers, Catholic and Protestant, rich and poor, are only one or two removes from the land.'

Just how ideological this view is can be judged from the fact that three of the plays — *Shadow and Substance*,

Katie Roche, and *Design for a Headstone* — are emphatically not peasant plays. The first is set in a parochial house in a small town and centres on a parish priest. The second is a strange exploration of the sexuality of a young woman in a small town. The third is set in a prison and features mostly IRA prisoners. But the need to insist that everyone, rural and urban, rich and poor, Catholic and Protestant can be made to fit in the same ideological nationalist frame because they are all just one or two removes from the land means that this basic fact must be ignored.

Equally, we also find Micheal O hAodha celebrating in 1961 the demise of a Dublin acting company at the Abbey: 'The advantage of a change-over, in recent years, from an all Dublin-born company, who could not have been so wonderful in realistic plays by Colum and Murray to a company drawn from the four provinces, has passed more or less unnoticed.' The unstated subtext of this comment is that, since the mainstream of Irish theatre is innately rural, having actors from Dublin in the national theatre is an obvious disadvantage.

Such assumptions had been more or less inherent in Irish cultural nationalism since the revival of the late nineteenth century. The form which the resurgence took was largely that of stark oppositions in which what was validly and properly Irish was whatever was furthest from English culture. If England was urban, Ireland had to be rural. If England was industrial, Ireland had to pastoral. Instead of looking clearly at Irish life in all its diversity, the new cultural movements tended to look for an Irishness that was defined in these ways, and that therefore excluded much of the reality of Irish urban life.

Excluded most dramatically, of course, was the urban North, the Ireland of shipyards and redbrick terraces, of linen mills and engineering works. 'Irish life', the mythic west as it came to be imagined, was quintessentially that of the West, a life of peasant simplicity, of the struggle of gnarled men with the landscape.

With or without censorship, this was a powerful ideological constraint. Likewise, what is really interesting about literary censorship is that the censors need not have bothered. A nationalist ideology in thrall to sentimental romanticism combined with an audience that was all too easily alienated to create a cultural vacuum. In this sense, Hubert Butler's comment in a 1949 article on *The County Libraries and Censorship* is important: 'The pressure towards censorship does not principally come, as Sean O'Faolain and his adversaries think, from either Church or State. It is entirely democratic and comes from the people.' Butler's point, of course, is not that censorship was a spontaneous expression of the will of the people, but that it must be understood as part of a broader failure on the part of the State and its governing ideology to take the job of creating a distinctive national culture at all seriously.

And writers could not do it on their own. A writer like O'Faolain who stayed in Ireland had the impossible task of trying to describe a barely-formed society. He and Frank O'Connor started out with the essentially nationalistic ambition of being Irish Gorkis or Turgenevs, honest explorers of a given national reality. But, as O'Connor subsequently wrote in *The Bell*, it became clear to them that even this destiny could not be theirs because the society they had chosen to depict had neither the depth nor the breadth of Russia in the nineteenth century. In Ireland, according to O'Connor, 'the moment a writer raises his eyes from the slums and cabins, he finds nothing but a vicious and ignorant middle-class, and for aristocracy the remnants of an English garrison'. It is no accident that both O'Faolain and O'Connor failed as novelists (novels need societies) and composed most successfully in the minor keys of the short story. 'Even today', confessed O'Faolain in his autobiography *Vive Moi!*, '"there is no such genre as the Irish Novel.'

For writers like O'Faolain, censorship was almost a back-handed compliment, in that it appeared to take their work more seriously than the society really did. As O'Faolain wrote in *The Bell*, writers were 'being treated as harmless maniacs, which is the worst situation for a political prisoner, and in that sense, all intellectuals in Ireland could be considered as political prisoners.'

The culture of the State was so unreceptive to any kind of serious literature that, banned or not, Irish books had virtually no market. Maurice Harmon in his biography of O'Faolain lists the sales figures for O'Faolain's *A Nest of Simple Folk*, which was not banned: six copies in Cork, 12 in Dublin, five in Limerick, three in Galway.

And the great irony of all of this is that the vacuum left by the State's cultural incompetence and the lack of an audience for serious Irish literature was filled by the very 'foreign trash' that the official ideology so despised. Hubert Butler analysed a County Library catalogue for 1936. He found that 94 per cent of the books issued were fiction, in itself a striking comment on the lack of interest in political, philosophical, social, and indeed, in a supposedly religious country, theological, issues. 'Yet', he wrote in 1949, 'among the novels I found no book, banned or unbanned, by Mr O'Faolain or Mr O'Connor, wheras there are 19 by Edgar Wallace and 51 by two ladies called Charlotte M. Braine and Effie A. Rowlands. These write about the sins of English peeresses. For example, to quote four consecutive entries from the catalogue, we have *Lady Brazil's Ordeal, Lady Damer's Secret, Lady Ethel's Whim, Lady Evelyn's Folly.'*

And this is the real point about the failure of Irish conservatism to create a sophisticated official culture of its own. It created, not even a genuine official art, but a vacuum which was filled precisely by the things that Irish culture was supposed to be guarded against. In Butler's words, there was 'not a displacement of Anglo-Saxon culture — it was never so strong and irresistible as it is now — but a progressive and appalling vulgarisation.'

Nationalist ideology, Gaelic revivalism and religious reaction in reality produced a culture whose real presiding goddesses were not Cathleen Ni Houlihan and the Virgin Mary but A Gal from Kalamazoo and Our Lady Evelyn of the Follies. That culture, with its contempt for cities, had nothing with which to absorb the new urban Ireland that began to develop from the late 1960s onwards. It had no great over-arching myth into which the children of the suburbs, fed on sex and drugs and rock and roll, might be absorbed. It was, paradoxically, the critics of nationalist orthodoxy, chief among them Sean O'Faolain, and the exiles, both internal and external, from de Valera's Ireland who managed, in spite of everything, to create over time what Irish political nationalism had virtually destroyed — a vibrant and distinctive national culture. The problem for Irish conservatism was that this national culture was, and has remained liberal, cosmopolitan and anti-clerical.

An Island Lightly
Moored

'Do you not feel that this island is moored only lightly to the sea-bed, and might be off for the Americas at any moment?'

Sebastian Barry, *Prayers of Sherkin*

Standing by the Cliffs of Moher, where the edge of Europe drops sheer into the Atlantic ocean, the American poet Wallace Stevens saw, not rock, sky or water, but the mythic origins of himself and mankind. 'This is not landscape', he wrote, '... this is my father or, maybe, / It is as he was,/ A likeness, one of the race of fathers: earth/ and sea and air.' And he was not alone in thinking of the rugged west coast of Ireland as a place outside history, a strange margin still illuminated by the sun that had risen at the dawn of European civilisation. The Aran Islands, and especially the Blasket Islands off the Kerry coast became for European culture generally, a mythic terrain, a place where Odysseus and Nestor still walked the earth and older verities remained true. The great Greek scholar George Thomson, who spent a great deal of time on the islands and edited Maurice O'Sullivan's account of his early life there, *Twenty Years A-Growing*, wrote of "the Homeric qualities in the life of the Blasket Island: The island of Ithaca had little to offer besides mountain pasture. 'It is a rough place', says Odysseus, 'but a fine nurse of men.' One might say the same of the Blasket Island."

The idea of an island had a special importance for the independent Irish state that was established in 1922. For the young country, the Blasket and Aran Islands had, as well as their echoes of Greek myth, a more specific aura of pre-history. They were part of the creation myth of the Irish state in which, as John Wilson Foster has put it 'the western island came to represent Ireland's mythic unity before the chaos of conquest... at once the vestige and the symbolic entirety of an undivided nation.' They were a past that would also be the future. Their supposed isolation had preserved them from corruption, kept their aboriginal Irishness intact through the long centuries of foreign rule. In this way of imagining an island, the sea was not an unstable and untrustworthy element but a stout and solid barrier, a fortification enclosing and protecting the culture within.

These two myths of the islands — as a survival of heroic archetypes, and as the point of origin of an independent Irish state — were not mutually exclusive and indeed they could be used to re-enforce each other, as in Robert Flaherty's famous ethnographic documentary film *Man of Aran*. The opening inscription for the film could be read almost word for word as a party political broadcast on behalf of Fianna Fail, which had just taken power when it had its premiere in Dublin: 'In this desperate environment, the man of Aran, because his independence is the most precious gift he can win from life, fights for his existence, bare though it may be.' That the cost of independence might be a bare and frugal existence was, after all, the message of Eamon de Valera, who graced the premiere with his presence.

In *Man of Aran*, the sea is imagined, not as an ever-changing, always unpredictable force, but as constant, unchanging, and perennial, a ring of timelessness that holds the mere day-to-day contingency of human life in an unbreakable grip.

This way of thinking about islands became a self-conscious part of the official ideology of the state. The books written by the Blasket Islanders — Maurice O'Sullivan, Tomas O'Crohan and Peig Sayers — were compiled, and placed on the school curriculum, as a record of a culture that had been, and would supposedly be again, emblematic of Gaelic Ireland itself.

In the one of those Blasket Island books drilled into the heads of generations of Irish school pupils, Peig Sayers's *An Old Woman's Reflections*, there is a snag in the story that threatens to unravel the entire weave of meaning. The book tells of a frugal, deeply religious, existence eked out from the rocks and the sea at the very edge of Europe. It is, in general terms, perfectly compatible with *Man of Aran.* But the myth, in Peig's telling, becomes strangely tongue-tied near the end.

This happens because another story — of emigration and depopulation, rather than of steadfast continuity, was already under way. Even before the first world war there were more Blasket islanders living in Springfield, Massachusetts, than on the Blaskets themselves. After it, when the fishing industry collapsed, America became not so much an alternative as a goal. In his diary in October 1922 Tomás O'Crohan, author of *The Islandman,* notes a conversation between a woman and her daughter after the currachs have returned for the third consecutive night without a fish caught. What, asks the mother, is there to keep the fishermen on the island? "They will have to leave for America so", says the daughter. "They do not find it easy to go there either" replies the mother, "They need to have fifty pounds — a sum no fisherman has when he has spent the last three years without making a single pound." As George Thomson put it, "in the old days, only those had emigrated who could not stay at home; now, only those stayed at home who could not emigrate."

This story breaks into *An Old Woman's Reflections* like interference from a foreign-language drama interrupting a sedate broadcast of Irish traditional music. The narrator's husband dies and no sooner has her son Muiris replaced the last sod over his grave, than he announces that he is off to America. On the morning of his departure,with his luggage ready and his papers on the table beside him, he stands stiff as a poker, his lips clamped, his thoughts somewhere between language and silence. Suddenly he turns on his mother who has been sitting in the corner, watching him with a secret eye. He takes out a package wrapped in brown paper and hands it abruptly to her. She opens it — it is the tricoloured flag of the new Irish state. 'Put that away', he says in a voice trembling with inarticulate emotion, 'in a place where neither moths nor flies can harm it! I have no business with it from this day out.'

The moment, passing between two members of a culture famed for the richness of its speech, is oddly inarticulate, and indeed, Peig herself was aware of it as such. She notes of her son that 'the words that jerked out of his mouth were all mixed up because of his emotion.' What was going on was, literally, hard to say. The hard-won abstract symbol of Irish nationhood — the flag — had proved to be useless to the living symbols of that same nationhood. Neither in Irish nor in English were there easy words for such a moment. It is the kind of history that could only be preserved as a photograph, the handing over of the national flag captured as an intimate and curiously inverted variation on end-of-empire ceremonies everywhere. When epochs like that of the Blaskets end (the islands were finally abandoned in 1953), the actual moment of death is marked by such awkward, unregarded moments.

✦ ✦ ✦ ✦ ✦

Seas don't separate, they join. The ocean is not a cultural barrier but a means of passage. Messages in bottles bob to the surface thousands of miles and many years from their points of origin. The waves throw objects onto the shore, and they lie mute and inscrutable, all the more alluring for their lack of context. They are found objects, so far from home, so out of place, that it is tempting to toss them back into the water again and forget that we ever saw them.

So it is with the Atlantic Ocean. On each of its shores, Ireland on one side, America on the other there are distorted echoes of the other, strange, disjointed bits of history from which the salt sea in between has bleached out the meaning. Let us pick up a few of them.

✦ ✦ ✦ ✦ ✦

After Sitting Bull was murdered by Native American policemen in 1890, they found a curious medal inscribed with the Latin words *Pro Petri Sede,* (For the Throne of Peter) around his neck. It had been presented by the Pope to an Irishman Myles Keogh for his part in the defence of the papal states against Garibaldi. Keogh afterwards joined the US Seventh Cavalry as a captain and, along with 115 other Irishmen intent on colonising Indian land, was killed at the Battle of Little Bighorn in 1876. Sitting Bull took his medal as a trophy, and cherished it until his death, a reminder, through the years of defeat and humiliation, of his people's one great victory over the white man.

On the other side of the Atlantic, another piece of jetsam was washed ashore. In the village of Asdee in North Kerry, behind the bar of the Jesse James Tavern, there is a notebook kept by a man who was parish priest there from the 1940s to the late 1960s. Convinced that the ancestors of Jesse and Frank James came from around the village, he collected local folklore about them. His notes read as follows:

Jesse James and Asdee

The most famous American outlaw of all time was the son of an Asdee man. Down along the Asdee River where it meets the river from the West is the place called Snugboro, where Jesse's father was born and lived until he emigrated shortly before the Famine times. At the foot of Martin Mulvihill's land is the mark of a house. Tradition has it that this is the site of the James homestead. The late Tom Linnane was able to recall that Ger O'Connor before him often heard his father telling how he once lived across the river from Jesse James's father. Tradition has it that the James family, though Protestant, once saved a priest from the hands of English priest-hunters, and we are told that an orchard once surrounded the house. Moss J. Mahoney of Asdee came across a pavement there some years ago while ploughing. Moss also had it from the late Thady Gorman, born 120 years ago, that the James family lived in Snugboro.

The name is to be found still in the North Kerry area, in Listowel to the present day, and until recent years in Beale. Jesse's father, after leaving the Shannon finally settled in Clay County, Missouri, and there on 5th September 1847, Jesse Woodson James, the future outlaw, was born. Way back in his father's country, the black ghost of Famine was treading the land..."

Snugboro

In West Asdee is Martin Mulvihill's farm. In Martin Mulvihill's farm are two fields, Upper and Lower Snugboro, ten acres in each. In Lower Snugboro, lived the Jameses. The fields have been ploughed several times, so nearly all the stones of their dwelling have been moved. Many have been used for building Martin Mulvill's dwelling, and his other out-offices. Martin Mulvihill, born on December 2nd 1926, told me this. (Father Ferris P.P.)

Blindness

The Jameses were Protestants. A servant girl of their's was going blind, and she went to the local holy well. She made a round there and got her sight. At the same time, her master had a horse gone blind. He took it to the holy well, and marched it around there several times. The horse got its sight, but James, its owner, got blind. (Martin Mulvihill, 6/4/1965)

Priest Hunting

In the penal days, a priest was saying Mass at the holy well when a yeoman came on him. He fled east and went into James's house. They told the yeoman that he had run past and was going before them. Being Protestants, they were believed. When the yeoman had gone away, the priest returned and finished his Mass at the well. (Martin Mulvihill, 6/4/1965)

Last James

When Jesse's father was leaving the locality, he looked back from the top of a hill and said "Goodbye Snugboro, and snug you were." (Martin Mulvihill)

Property

The Fitzgeralds owned James's farm after the Jameses's going, and owned all the land down to the shore, so it is likely that the Jameses also owned it all before them. It was afterwards the Hickeys came and divided all the land into farms. (Martin Mulvihill)

Smugglers

Father Ferris, PP here in 1943, heard in his early years that the Jameses used pay their workmen every Saturday evening, each man with a stick of tobacco as long as himself. He does not remember the name of his informant and he has heard no one mentioning it recently. We can deduce some things from this tradition and others:

1. It is possible that the Jameses were smuggling tobacco.

2. It is probable that they were smuggling other things as well.

3. They were popular amongst the people. The legend of their saving a priest showed this.

4. The item above about the last James saying a wistful goodbye to Snugboro as he was leaving goes to show that they left unwillingly.

5. Here, trouble with the revenue authorities may
have caused their departure. (Jesse James
Tavern, October 1964)

Jesse James is still lovingly remembered in his ancestral parish
of Asdee where his grandfather was born. The only two photos
of Jesse in existence hang proudly in the Church there.
Furthermore, each year a commemoration Mass, is celebrated
on the 3rd of April, the anniversary of his death. Recently the
parish has been at considerable expense. If anyone wishes to
join in honouring Jesse's memory, let him send a subscription
to: The Parish Priest, Asdee, County Kerry, Ireland."

✦ ✦ ✦ ✦ ✦

Nothing is more fixed than graves, and there is no more
visceral attachment to a place than the pull that people
feel towards the spot where their ancestors are buried. But
it is not for nothing that the phrase 'coffin ships' has a place
in the Irish lexicon. To someone who knew nothing of Irish
history, that phrase might suggest the strange image of a
coffin under full sail, ploughing through the Atlantic
waves, searching for a place to be buried. And such an
image would not be entirely absurd, for there are, on both
sides of the Ocean, graves that are far from fixed.

When he was a small boy, walking after dark through
the village on the Great Blasket, Sean O'Crohan and the
other children used to scare each other by saying 'the old
Spanish woman will come before us tonight!'. The ghost
they conjured was a memory nearly four centuries old, of
a woman's body washed up on the island after the wreck
of the *Santa Maria de la Rosa*, a ship of the Spanish
Armada. According to local traditions, she was a rich lady
with gold rings on her fingers and gold bracelets on her
wrists, and she was buried at Castle Point. In the
twentieth century, an old islander could still point out the
unmarked grave to the young O'Crohan. The strange

catastrophe that threw an exotic Spanish woman up onto the coast of the Blaskets had taken root in the very soil.

Ninety years ago, a poem in Irish, *Ochón! A Dhonncha*, was published in Patrick Pearse's periodical *An Claidheamh Solúis*, with a translation into English by Pearse himself. It is a cry of anguish from the heart of a father whose small son has been drowned and, to anyone reading it, it seems to speak with all the immense dignity of an immemorial tradition. It conforms to literary conventions of lamentation that stretched back at least three centuries, and to an Irish custom of keening the dead that is older than any literature. Between the covers of Pearse's nationalist and Gaelic revivalist journal, it seems the most vivid and gripping proof of the existence of an unbroken culture, a tradition that had survived both centuries and catastropes with its purity intact.

Except, however, for two lines in the first verse:

Da mbeadh an codladh so i gCill na Dromad ort
no in uaigh san Iarthar
mo bhrón do bhogfadh, cé gur mhór mo dhocar,
is ni bheinn id' dhiaidh air.

(If this sleep was on you in Cill na Dromad
or some grave in the West
it would soften my sorrow, though great my affliction,
and I'd not complain.)

Why would a grave in the West of Ireland be a comfort? Because the poem was written, not in Kerry, but in Springfield, Massachusetts, and it is the lament of an emigrant for an American future that has been blighted. Its author Padraig O hEigeartaigh was born in Iveragh in 1871, emigrated to America twelve years later, moved to Springfield when he was twenty and spent the rest of his life there, working in the Charles F. Lynch Clothing

Company. And he wasn't the inheritor of an immemorial tradition of Gaelic culture. He learned to read and write Irish from a book of poems he picked up in the States. His poem for his dead son, this lament for the little American boy buried in St Michael's cemetery in Springfield came, not out of a rich past but out of an emigrant's need for something to take with him into an unknown future in a foreign land. It was made possible, not by continuity but by displacement. And yet it is, for all that, the last great Gaelic lament, not as Pearse must have hoped, evidence of a culture's survival, but a desperately moving dying echo of the old world in the new.

◆ ◆ ◆ ◆ ◆

In 1866, 200 members of the Fenian Brotherhood invaded Canada, carrying a green flag with a golden harp embroidered onto it. Their plan was to conquer the colony, and then propose a swap to the British Empire, offering to give back Canada in return for a free Ireland. The invasion lasted three days before the Fenians were forced to retreat back into the United States. One of the wounded men they carried over the border with them was Timothy McCoy, who in 1848, as a child of three, had emigrated from Glyn, County Limerick. The family had settled in a Gaelic-speaking community in upper New York State, and Timothy McCoy had grown up as a passionate Irish Catholic nationalist. After the failed invasion of Canada, he married an Irish woman, Cathrin Fitzpatrick from Johnstown, County Kilkenny, and became chief of police in Saginaw, Michigan.

Their son Tim grew up there with two sets of stories in his ears. On the one hand, there was Ireland. The atmosphere of the house was, as he recalled in his memoirs, *Tim McCoy Remembers the West*, 'nationalistically Irish and devoutly Catholic'. Although his mother was 20 when she emigrated to America, his father 'always seemed more Irish to me, though I imagine that when she was young she must have been the typical colleen: dainty, pretty, with dark auburn hair, a rosy complexion and an ever present twinkle in her eye.' And on the other hand, there were Indians. When he lay on the floor beside the wood-burning stove, he heard the adults talking of 'everything from leprechauns to Michigan's frontier days'. One Irish neighbour told him such tales of wild Indians that he was often afraid to go to bed.

As soon as he could, he ran off to the West, to Nebraska and Wyoming. He became a cowboy and 'it was through cowboying that my association with the Indians began, an association which proved my entry into Hollywood.' When he first met Indians, Arapahos and Shoshonis, his reaction to them was the same as that of George Thompson to the Blasket islanders or of Robert Flaherty to the Aran islanders: 'they could not help but strike me as exotic and interesting. Being at heart a romantic, I was intrigued by the possibility that, having come from an unencumbered, natural state, the Indians were able to look upon the world as we must all have seen it before the influence of 'civilisation', before that time when we forever lost a firm grip upon our own, probably common, roots.'

But just as he encountered his first Indians, he also fell in with another Irishman, a cattleman called Irish Tom. His proper name was Thomas Walsh 'and he was raised, much as my father had been, in an American Gaelic-speaking community, as a result of which he had a brogue which could have been rent with a cleaver.' From his habit of singing traditional Gaelic airs to Irish Tom's cattle, Tim McCoy acquired the nickname 'Irish Tom's Canary'. But while he was singing his Irish songs to the cattle, he also linked up with another cow-puncher, an Arapaho called Buffalo Lodge. From him, he learned the Arapaho sign-language. The image of the two of them, way out West, the child of a dying Gaelic culture and the child of a dying Arapaho culture, singing the airs of half-forgotten laments and speaking in silent signs, comes from the history of an island but lightly moored to the sea-bed.

Later, visiting an Arapaho reservation, McCoy joined in their dances, and felt himself at one with the chief, Chiatee, called in English, Goes In Lodge: 'I looked at him and it suddenly seemed that the cultural allegiances which might once have kept us from understanding one another had vanished. It was somehow necessary to both of us that I be with him and among the Arapahoes.' He began to learn the tribe's dances, and became so adept that Chiatee and his friends lent him their costumes, and bet on him in dancing competitions against younger tribesmen. 'Entered as a visiting southern Arapaho, I was not readily recognised as a white man cowboy.' Later, among a tribe of Bannocks Indians, McCoy used Arapaho sign language. 'Bannocks flocked from every direction to see an Irish Arapaho talk to them in a language many of them could understand.'

Staying with the Arapaho and learning their language, Irish Tom's Canary saw them in almost exactly the same way that Robert Flaherty would see McCoy's sea-divided Gaelic cousins, the Aran islanders, 20 years later. Flaherty imagined them as a people ennobled by stoicism in the face of inevitable defeat. In *Man of Aran,* the opening inscription stresses the archetypal, and essentially fatalistic, nature of the islander's struggle to wrest an existence from inscrutable nature: 'It is a fight from which he will have no respite until the end of his indomitable days or until he meets his master, the sea.' This timeless, mythic stoicism is also what McCoy saw in the Arapaho: 'The Arapahoes accepted reality without question and looked upon disaster and good fortune with much the same stoicism. It was, they reasoned, all part of the Great Mystery, the nature of which was amply explained by its name'.

In 1922, just as an independent Ireland was coming into existence and searching for its myths of origin, Tim McCoy began to play his own part in the mythologising of both his Arapaho friends and the men who shot them like dogs. Hollywood had no place for such a richly ambivalent figure as an Irish Arapaho, and McCoy became a cowboy again. He got a job with Famous Pictures-Lasky (later called Paramount) as a supplier of Indian extras for Wild West films. By 1926, he was himself a Hollywood star, playing a white cowboy hero in 16 silent Westerns, and 32 talkies. He also mounted the last Buffalo Bill-style Wild West Show, *Tim McCoy's Wild West and Rough Riders of the World*. When television came in the 1950s, he did his own shows, 'telling Indian legends and... telling the audience about the real history of the West.' But what, in a story that runs from the Famine to the Fenian invasion of Canada, through an Irish Arapaho, and to the making of media myths, is the real history?

Meanwhile, on the far side of the Atlantic, the Blasket islanders had become dead Indians. 'It's a sad occasion', says Peig Sayers in her book, 'when a person leaves for America; it's like death for only one out of a thousand ever again returns to Ireland.' But, although it seemed that way to communities on the west coast, emigration is not a death. Communities, even cultures, die. But lives go on. Even if the individuals never return, their ideas and dreams do.

And as the idea of the island as a theme park of mythic Irishness faded away, the Irish built new kinds of compounds to house fantasies of an authentic past. The brochure for Drumcoura City cowboy ranch near Ballinamore, County Leitrim offers an invitation to 'Live the Legend of the Old West', to have 'the ultimate western experience right here in Ireland'. Drumcoura City, on the shores of Lough Gowna, is an entertainment complex of log cabins and bunk houses, where tourists can pay to dress up as cowboys and cowgirls. But the legend of the Old West is no longer to be found, as it was for Wallace Stevens or George Thompson, on the Blaskets or the Cliffs of Moher. It is the American west, not the Irish west, that is the landscape of dreams, where you can 'learn how to become a real cowboy or cowgirl', and feel at home on the cattle range.

But even these dreams tend to impinge on real life. In January 1997, for a few days, Drumcoura City ceased to be entertaining. In Bawnboy, near Belturbet, County Cavan, a German man, Gerrit Isenborger, who had worked as a 'cowboy' on the ranch, shot and wounded three officials from the county sheriff's office, who had come to evict him from a cottage belonging to Michael Hehle, the Austrian who had built Drumcoura. He then held the police at bay with his rifle and shotgun. The tabloid *Star* newspaper reported the siege under the headline 'Sheriff Shot in Cowboy Showdown'.

✦ ✦ ✦ ✦ ✦

The Blasket Islanders themselves dreamed of flotsam and jetsam. They grew tired of being a living museum, the objects of tourist fantasies. One of them, Eibhlis Ní Shuilleabhain, wrote that "Visitors going in and going out of our house talking and talking and they on their holidays and they at home having a comfortable house and no worry during winter or summer would never believe the misfortune on this island, no school nor comfort, no road to success, no fishing... everything so dear and so far away. Surely people could not live on air or sunshine."

But as well as being objects of fantasy, the islanders had fantasies of their own. With no road to success, they dreamed of American bounty washing its way across the waves to them. Tomás O'Crohan, in his diary, recorded the hope of an islandman in 1922 that 'Maybe there would be another war too and God would load a fine valuable vessel over in the United States and would steer her onto Lochar Rock as he steered the *Quebra,* a wrecked ship that had provided a fine crop of salvage.'

God answered these prayers, but not quite in the way the islanders might have imagined. The Blasket islanders went to America, mostly to Springfield, Massachusetts, but America also came to the bigger island of which the Blaskets were once an idealised emblem. Movies and multinational companies, dreams and dresses, consumer durables and fizzy drinks, ideas, aspirations and lifestyles, all drifted ashore, released by the wreckage of nationalist myths.

This is the way with Irish culture. The surrounding seas keep nothing out and nothing in. They ebb and flow, carrying things and people back and forth until it is hard to say where they began and where they might end. What was washed up on the shores of Ireland was often, weathered and sea-changed, what had been cast adrift from them a generation earlier.

Looking for a mainland when their home became uninhabitable, the people of the Blasket islands off the Kerry coast believed they would find a more hospitable landfall across the Atlantic Ocean than across the Blasket Sound. In many ways, their judgement of where the mainland lay showed the navigational astuteness to be expected of a sea-going community. From the America which they now inhabit, Ireland is an offshore island, semi-detached, outlying, a clear field for fantasies.

Emigration and
Irish Culture

No Place Like Home

The last of that immigrant generation have all but slipped away, but the effect of the broad strokes of the comedians and caricaturists has been to tamper with memory. Unthinkingly the descendants accept the stereotypes, and squeeze their ancestors into the narrow and rather condescending mould that others have created for them.

Ruth Gay, *Unfinished People*

A hundred years ago, in May 1897, an Irish Fair was held at the Grand Central Palace on Lexington Avenue, New York, to raise funds for an Irish Palace Building, intended to contain a library, a shooting range and a riding school. The most popular exhibit was a giant topographical map of Ireland. In a long, rectangular room, surmounted by a huge green shamrock and surrounded by five columned archways, the map was spread across the floor. It was divided into 32 parts, each representing the exact contours of a county. But the special attraction of the map was that each of these 'counties' had been filled with 'the veritable Irish soil of the county... duly attested as truly genuine'. For ten cents, the visitor to the fair could walk the length and breadth of the island. The Irish immigrant could feel under foot the land itself, the literal ould sod.

As the New York Irish World reported, 'many a pathetic scene is witnessed daily'. One day an 80 year-old Fermanagh woman called Kate Murphy paid her ten cents and stepped across the coastline and made for her native county. She knelt down and kissed the soil, "then, crossing herself, proceeded to say her prayers, unmindful of the crowd around her. While thus kneeling, a photographer took a flashlight picture of her. The flash was a revelation to the simple hearted creature, who seemed to think it a light from heaven, and was awed into reverential silence. When she finally stepped off the Irish soil, she sighed sadly and clung to the fence, still gazing at 'Old Ireland'. She kept looking backward as she walked away, as if bidding a long farewell."

The strange, haunting quality of this event has much to do with its apparent confusion of time and place. It confuses time because, though it happened a century ago, it seems to belong so obviously to the end of the 20th century: the virtual reality of the re-created Ireland, nature (the real soil 'duly attested as truly genuine') become culture (an exhibit framed, packaged and commodified available at ten cents a throw), intense personal experiences played out in the artificial glow of camera flashes, signs taken for wonders. A country has become a heritage attraction long before such an idea ought to have gained currency.

And it confuses place because, in a room in a city in another continent, there is still an overpowering sense of Ireland. The very stuff of the land has become, not less but more tangible, not more abstract but more real. The soil trodden heedlessly so many millions of times, the earth that was scraped off boots or washed off potatoes, has acquired the awesome magic of authenticity. It matters deeply that the soil was not scooped from a garden in Queens of or even shipped in a job lot from Dublin, but carefully gathered in each county.

And those confusions of time and place are central to Irish experience. For the Ireland of the 1990s, there is no straight line of historical development leading from the past to the present. The present generation in Ireland itself is faced with experiences it regards as new — globalisation, multiple identities, imagining society as multiracial and multicultural, living in a media-saturated universe where reality and image are often indistinguishable. And, on the island itself, those experiences are indeed new. But, for previous generations of Irish people, they are not new at all. The Irish men and women who lived in New York and London, in Chicago and Glasgow, have gone through it already. Not just our present but our future is their past. The grand narrative of a society moving from the pre-modern to the modern to the post-modern, breaks down in Ireland.

Consider, for instance, the question of tolerance for other cultures. One of the great paradoxes of Irish history after the foundation of the State is the complete contradiction between the expectation, on the one hand, that Irish people had a right to emigrate to wherever they could, and on the other, the great reluctance to allow immigration into Ireland, even in the extreme circumstances of Jewish refugees fleeing the Holocaust. It is as if there were at one and the same time two Irelands: a pre-modern one contained on the island itself which assumed that the natural state of a culture was one of monolithic purity, and a post-modern one outside the island, able to cope with the global intermingling of race, ethnicity and religion. These two Irelands do not succeed each other in a logical chronological order. The more open precedes the less open.

Thus, for instance, in the 1920s there were no fewer than 22 films dealing with relations between the Irish and the Jews in America. The depiction of romances between Irish girls and Jewish boys was almost a stock-in-trade of popular drama. The vogue was inspired by Anne Nichols's 1922 comedy, *Abie's Irish Rose*, in which a Jewish boy and an Irish Catholic girl, afraid to tell their parents that they are in love, are married by a Methodist minister. It had 2,327 performances, one of the longest runs in the history of Broadway, and was also turned into a novel (1927), a radio serial (1942), and a movie (1946).

Yet, 23 years after *Abie's Irish Rose* opened on Broadway, the idea of allowing any significant number of Jews into

Ireland was still anathema. Writing in 1945, S.A. Roche, secretary of the Department of Justice in Dublin, reviewed Irish government policy on the reception of Jewish refugees during the Holocaust: 'The immigration of Jews is generally discouraged. The wealth and influence of the Jewish community in this country appear to have increased considerably in recent years and there is some danger of exciting opposition and controversy if this tendency continues. As Jews do not become assimilated with the native population, like other immigrants, any big increase in their numbers might create a social problem.' Roche subsequently wrote that Jews 'do not assimilate with our own people but remain a sort of colony of a world-wide Jewish community. This makes them a potential irritant in the body politic and has led to disastrous results from time to time in other countries.' An image of Irishness that was a commonplace of popular culture in New York was unimaginable in Ireland itself.

The same is true of Irish contact with other races. Irish-American racism has a long and dishonourable history, but there is some reason to believe that later Irish emigrants were more racist than their predecessors. In pre-1870s New York, about a quarter of all Chinese men were married to Irish women. Delinquent Irish and African American teenagers were brought together in the House of Refuge, a New York reformatory, and often formed lasting relationships. In 1853, the *New York Times* reported that black and Irish waiters had formed a union and gone on strike together.

In the 1840s and 1850s, Irish and black people mixed freely in the Five Points district of New York, bounded by the Bowery to the east and Broadway to the west. Graham Hodges has noted that in the local bars and dance halls 'Irish and black revellers danced, sang and courted to popular melodies composed from European and African rhythms.' In Ned Buntline's 1850 novel, *The G'Hals of New York*, an Irishman 'commenced humming, in a low tone, the Negro melody of *Mary Blane*' but 'there was nothing in this to arrest particular attention.'

Charles Dickens, visiting one of the Five Points bars, noted that "In the negro melodies you catch a strain of what has been metamorphosed from such Scotch or Irish tunes, into somewhat of a chiming, jiggish air." Accompanied by two policemen on a visit to Peter Williams's tavern in Five Points, Dickens was astonished to see Irish and black men and women dancing, drinking and making love. After Dickens, as Graham Hodges puts it, 'no popular construction of Five Points was complete without a description of a love affair between a black man and an Irish woman.'

In 1850, George Foster, in a guide to the Five Points district, noted the frequency of intermarriage between black American men and Irish women. In one home, for instance, there were two inter-racial couples, John de Poyster, a black labourer, and his wife Brigid, from Ireland, sharing the house with John Francis, a black man from Virginia and his Irish wife Susan.

And yet, in the early decades of the Irish State, not alone was the presence within the nation of black or Chinese people — let alone the idea of sexual relations between Irish women and black men — unimaginable, but even black-influenced music was widely regarded as intolerable. The Gaelic League, launching a renewed anti-jazz campaign in 1934 declared that "It is this music and verse that the Gaelic League is determined to crush... Its influence is denationalising in that its references are to things foreign to Irishmen: that it is the present-day instrument of social degradation is all too plain, even in Ireland. That was the reason for the re-launching of the anti-jazz campaign, the reason it received the blessing of the church and the approval of the State."

Only recently, in the wake of the collapse of Irish nationalism and Irish Catholicism, and in the context of the Republic's utter openness to global economic and cultural forces, has it become possible for the people who still live on the island to catch up with the experiences of their great-grandparents in the cities of America and, to a lesser extent Britain. Thus, the best description of Ireland's place in the world at the end of the 20th century is this description, not of the present, but of the past of the Irish community in New York, given by Ronald H. Bayer and Timothy J. Meagher in their 1996 book *The New York Irish:*

'Throughout their history in New York, the Irish have been at the border of the ins and outs, interpreting one to the other, mediating, sometimes including, sometimes excluding. They have been both victim and victimiser, 'other' and definer of the 'other', and, paradoxically, sometimes played both roles simultaneously.'

What is history for the New York Irish is news for the Irish Irish, balanced, in a global society, between the ins the outs, the victims and the victimisers. There is a sense of moving back to the future, of the newest and most astonishing changes — mass media, virtual reality, the fusion of cultures — being a repetition of what is, in the history of emigrants, old hat. There is also a sense that what is most alien, most foreign, is also a kind of homecoming.

◆ ◆ ◆ ◆ ◆

The sense, in the Ireland of the 1990s, of things coming home is related to the sense that in our culture 'home' is a word that had no meaning without 'away'. Kate Murphy's passion and prayers, her outpouring of emotion at the touch of her native soil, are possible in New York, not in Fermanagh. The sense of belonging to a place has often been, in modern Irish culture, in direct proportion to one's distance from it: the further away 'home' is, the larger it looms. Home was not the place you were living in, but whatever was least like it. In the Irish countryside, people longed for foreign cities. In foreign cities, they re-imagined an Ireland that had not interested them when they lived there.

Even in traditional Irish culture, there is no easy sense of *home* as a natural, uncomplicated state of grace, as something that can be taken for granted. The great *sean nós* singer Joe Heaney used to sing a traditional song called *Peigín is Peadar*. He would preface it with a story in which a poor man is six months married when his wife falls pregnant. She tells him that, with a child coming, he will have to go away and earn some money. He gets work with a farmer 20 miles away, and agrees to stay for seven years. At the end of the seven years, he has forgotten his home, and stays another seven. And at the end of that time, he stays another seven.

After 21 years, he remembers that he has a home 20 miles away, but has forgotten that when he left his wife was expecting a child. He tells the farmer's wife that he is leaving to go home. She bakes him a cake to take with him, while her husband offers him a choice. Either he can have his wages for the 21 years, or he can have what Joe Heaney in his beautiful Connemara English called 'three advices', one for every seven years he spent with them. The man chooses the advices: whatever way the road is, never take the short cut; never sleep a night in a house where there is an old man married to a young woman; never do anything at night you'd be sorry for next morning.

He leaves, and passing a lake, he sees a short-cut. He takes it but remembers the first advice and turns back. Later he learns that two robbers have killed a man walking on that short-cut. He arrives at a house and, looking in the door, sees a young woman serving supper to an old man. They offer him a bed for the night, but he sleeps in the barn instead. At midnight, a young man calls to the house, and he and the young woman murder the old man. In the morning, the man reaches home and finds his wife in bed with a bearded man. He reaches behind the door for the hatchet they always kept there, and is about to kill them both when he thinks of the third advice. He asks his wife who the man is and is told that it is his son, born three months after he left. They cut the cake for breakfast and inside find his wages for 21 years labour.

Such stories are as old as *The Odyssey*, but they were still being sung by a generation in Ireland that is only now passing. They remind us that *home* is not, in the experience of ordinary people throughout history, just a familiar place, something to be taken for granted. It is something that has to be worked for and achieved, a goal that can be reached only by circumnavigating, with help and luck, ferocious dangers, unpredictable treacheries both outside yourself and within your own heart. And you need to be armed with advices, with warnings and incantations that form invisible threads for you to follow. The advices that we hope will lead us safe home are what we call a culture.

One of the things that culture reminds us of is that home is much more than a name we give to a dwelling place. It is also a whole set of connections and affections, the web of mutual recognition that we spin around ourselves and that gives us a place in the world. Older languages tend to contain this idea within themselves. In Irish, the terms *sa mbaile* and *sa bhaile,* the equivalents of the English *at home,* are never used in the narrow sense of home as a dwelling. They imply, instead, that wider sense of a place in the world, a feeling of belonging that is buried deep within the word's meaning.

It is particularly true of Irish culture that the imagination itself is inextricable from the idea of home, usually made powerful by the act of leaving it. Looking at 111 letters to and from Irish emigrants to Australia in the second half of the nineteenth century, David Fitzpatrick found that *home* had much more than a literal meaning, often 'evoking an alternative world of recollection and imagination'. In the network of recollection and imagination — remembering the past and inventing the future — that makes a culture, there's no place like home.

A history of emigration gave to Irish culture a particularly sharp realisation of the fact that a home is much more than a house. Fitzpatrick found the word *home* 229 times, on average more than twice in each letter. One woman writing from Queensland used the term 30 times in three letters. And significantly the word was used far more often by the exiles than by those who remained in Ireland. Eighty one per cent of the occurrences were in letters from Australia, just 19 per cent in letters from Ireland.

In most cases, *home* was not used to refer to a house, but to a whole social world. Fitzpatrick lists the shades of meaning in these letters: a dwelling-place, a household, a neighbourhood, a country, an unspecified place, an address, a place with special characteristics, a place with special emotional associations, a place to return to. 'Home', he found, 'was not only a symbol of shelter and comfort, but also a scene of sociability and match-making.' Yet, when the emigrants talked of 'home' in Australia, these larger associations were mostly absent. Adjectives suggesting warmth, comfort or sociability tended not to be used. *Home* came to mean just a household, 'typically used as part of a mundane dichotomy with school, shop or work-place.'

Home became, in Irish culture, not so much the place you were as the place you wanted to be, a place as much imagined as remembered or experienced. 'Home in Ireland', writes Fitzpatrick of the emigrants' letters, 'was both a real and an imagined location. As an economic unit it continued to affect the fortunes of Irish Australians through the transfer of money and gifts as well as the organisation of further movement. As an imagined location, it sometimes took the form of a dwelling, but equally often of a household or neighbourhood buzzing with banter and gossip. As a symbol of comfort, stability and usually affection, it provided an important source of solace for those facing the taxing and insecure life of the emigrant.'

This imagined, symbolic home became, when it was re-imported into Ireland, the touchstone of both politics and religion. And it is also the link between politics and religion, the thread that bound Catholicism and nationalism, Protestantism and unionism, together. Because the idea of a homeland was so steeped in emotion and yearning, it came to be identified with a spiritual home, a land of milk and honey, a paradise both earthly and unearthly. Both Irish traditions — the Gaelic and Catholic one and the British and Protestant one — came to believe that only by making their home territory spiritually pure, dominated by the righteous believers in their own religion, could it be a fitting symbol on earth of the holy homeland in their heads.

And thus a yearning that began as nostalgia has ended, in our own time, as bloody conflict. The roots of the feeling, in exile, in the act of going out into the world and living with people of different races and languages and traditions, were forgotten. A way of writing, of inventing and of imagining, became a way of reading, of imposing, of defending. The job of culture is to make it into a way of writing again, and, appropriately, it is writers who have been searching for ways to do this.

✦ ✦ ✦ ✦ ✦

One way of envisaging that task is to think of a culture as a way of measuring and to remember that Ireland has, in recent decades, changed its system of measurement. When I was ten, we started to learn the metric system of measurement at school. Where before we had measured everything by British imperial standards — walking for miles, drinking pints of milk, measuring out the goals for football on the basis that every large step was a yard —

now we were to realise that there was a whole other system, neater, more logical, more redolent of the future.

Though we did not understand this at the time, the decision that we should learn about metres and litres was itself highly political, a symbol that we would no longer be ex-colonials, shuffling around imperial prison-yards on shackled feet, but Europeans. Ireland was preparing to join the European Economic Community, and we were entranced with the idea that some great transformation was on the way. Once, part of my school homework was to measure in metres and centimetres the ordinary objects around the house: the height of the door, the width of the table, the depth of the kitchen sink. And even writing down their dimensions in this new language of a glossy, standard Europe, the objects themselves seemed transformed, no longer their mundane selves, but promising and full of allure.

For me, part of that allure was a simple but radiant image. We learned that the metre was a standard measure of distance, and that every metre we measured was a copy of a prototype metre-long metal bar held in the International Bureau of Weights and Measures in Paris. It was a nice thing to know. There was something comforting about feeling that every distance you could ever traverse was a version of the same distance, that every step you could take was in step with all the others around the world. That unseen, inscrutable length of platinum and iridium in a Parisian vault seemed to guarantee that something, at least, would always be exact and unchanging. Behind all the transformations of Ireland at the time, the epic shift from a traditional and rural society to a modern and urban one seemed to lie this new guarantee of continuity and certainty.

That comforting idea — that everything could change and still be continuous — was one way of imagining Ireland. And as I grew up, the metric system suggested another. It came from the fact that even after we had joined the European Economic Community and adopted the new metric system, we all continued to ignore the measurements and use the old ones. Even the Gaelic Athletic Association, the guardian of traditional Irish games like Gaelic football, converted yards to metres and started to call a 50, the free kick that you get when one of the opposing players puts the ball beyond his own end-line, a 45. But everyone went on thinking of it as a 50.

To this day, we drink pints of beer, complain that the beach is miles away, ask for so many square yards of carpet. To this day, if I am told something in metric figures, I have to work out what it would be in imperial figures before it has any meaning for me. And that is a second way of imagining Ireland: that if a culture is about the way people measure things, the residue of an old way of measuring hangs around long after it has ceased to have an official existence.

But there is a third way of imagining Ireland suggested by the metric system, and it struck me recently when I discovered the disturbing fact that the way of fixing the length of the metre has, after all, changed. The platinum and iridium bar may still be in Paris, but it is no longer the ultimate definition of distance. These days, distance is measured, quite literally, in time. Since 1983, length is measured by the clock, not the measuring-tape. A metre is no longer a version of a precious metal bar in Paris but the distance that light travels in a given infinitesimal fraction of a second. The ultimate point of reference is no longer physically present, no longer fixed and immutable, but itself in frantic motion, a blur of light that covers 300 million metres a second. It is itself a journey.

These three lessons from the metric system each contain a truth about Ireland. It is a country is which change itself provides the only possible continuity. It is a culture whose way of measuring things are often unofficial, vestigial and unexplicit, even to insiders. And it is, above, all, a country whose journeys can no longer be measured by fixed standards, but that have to be gauged by their relation to other, imaginative journeys.

It used to be that at all points around the globe, in Boston or in Glasgow, in New York or in London, in Sydney or in Berlin, the emigrant's distance could be measured in relation to a fixed, unchanging standard called Ireland. Somewhere beyond the waters, locked away in a sealed and sacred vault as an ultimate point of reference, there was a fixed, unchanging length of space, an island in the Atlantic standing firm against the waves and wind. Every step the traveller took could be, imaginatively at least, measured in distance to or from that remembered home.

Now, Ireland itself must be measured not with the metres that derive from a fixed, immutable length of metal in Paris, but from the passage of light through time. Ireland has started to imagine itself in the way photographers imagine the world, measuring distance by the motion of light rather than by a fixed, unmoving object. Its imagined metres and centimetres are the marks of human journeys across the landscape. And it is driven by a desire as old as humanity itself but one that is especially strong in the 1990s world where global connections have made the world no less inscrutable and no more homely. It is the desire for safe passage, the desire for an endless ball of thread with which to mark our way in the labyrinth so that we can always retrace our steps, the desire for true lines through a map of the world.

◆ ◆ ◆ ◆ ◆

In November 1995, the Minor Planet Centre in Cambridge, Massachusetts decided to name Minor Planet 5029, an asteroid recently discovered somewhere between Mars and Jupiter, "Ireland". Minor Planet Ireland is far away and virtually invisible to the naked eye and almost nothing is known about its composition. It bears, in other words, a similar relationship to the terrestrial Ireland as the emergent Ireland of imaginative connections does to the physical Ireland in the Atlantic. Spinning in the dark, held in place by the pull of invisible gravity, it is still solid, full of possibilities, and, perhaps, habitable.

In another sense, though, Minor Planet Ireland is not so dreamily comforting. Ireland has long had its human satellites, its exiled communities orbiting the motherland. But it is not so long since people thought that all the planets went round the earth, and had to suffer the psychic shock of finding that it was the other way around. These days, it gets harder to shake off the thought, absurd but insistent, that Minor Planet Ireland, the distant place called after a familiar one, is not the imagined asteroid but the real, green island that used to be at the edge of Europe.

Unsuitables From a Distance: The Politics of *Riverdance*

In November 1995, something new happened in a small, often esoteric, corner of Irish culture. At the Oireachtas, the annual festival of Gaelic-language performance, the prize for *sean nós* singing — the coveted Corn Uí Riada — was won by Mairead Ni Oistin for her renditions of *Donncha Ban* and *Barr an tSleibhe*. Accepting her trophy, she said "Mothaim an chaoi cheanna is a mhothaigh me mi Mhean Fomhair nuair a bhuaigh Baile Atha Cliath an All-Ireland." ("I feel the same way I did in September when Dublin won the All-Ireland".) In every previous year, this would have been a baffling statement: when Dublin won the All-Ireland, *sean nós* singers, who were, by definition, from rural Ireland, did not feel happy. But the winner was not, in fact, trying to say that she was browned off with her victory. Her speech made easy sense because she was the first native Dubliner even to win the Corn Uí Riada.

Small as this event was, it had large resonances. For what it meant was that one of the most delicate and extraordinary forms of traditional Irish art — the baroque, bardic vocal style, full of awesome complexities and sensational pleasures — had survived its transplantation from a Gaelic and rural world to an urban, cosmopolitan city. What it meant was that though traditional forms must inevitably change when they are removed from the world in which they grew, they do not necessarily have to die. The content may not be the same, but the form can, perhaps, survive. And if a form as delicate and complex as

143

sean nos could go down the mean city streets without withering in the noise and haste, there was no reason why the much rougher form of Irish dancing could not merely survive transplantation, but put down new roots. It had, after all, a long history in the rough-and-tumble of Irish unsettlement.

In Cobh, the port from which Irish emigrants embarked for the New World, the cheap boarding houses where the steerage class passengers waited for their passage, became notoriously overcrowded. For those left without a bed, there was, however, a well-known device for getting one. For a few pence, you could get a musician to come in off the street, and strike up a lively tune. Some of those in bed would be unable to resist the urge to get up and dance. And while they reeled around the floor, you could make a dash for the bed. At worst, you could lie down for as long as the dancing continued. At best, if you were strong enough, possession was nine points of the law.

There is something of this mixture of gaiety and desperation, of this dancing on the edge of destruction, about *Riverdance*, the phenomenally successful Irish dance show in which the razzle-dazzle and the spectacle, the sexiness and the celebration, are inextricable from a narrative of emigration, displacement and loss. Part of the show's energy, its almost frantically compulsive drive, was reminiscent of the stock scene in the old westerns where the baddie fires his gun at his victim's feet and says 'Hey, gringo, let's see you dance'. If the feet stop moving, if they don't rise high enough from the floor, there will be a howl of pain.

It does not seem accidental that *Riverdance* came shortly after another huge international theatrical success from Ireland that also depended crucially on a poignant conjunction of dancing and despair, Brian Friel's *Dancing At Lughnasa*. In its central moment, the pain of three sisters in 1930s Donegal bursts forth in a wild dance to the music of a ceili band playing *The Mason's Apron* on the radio, a dance whose rhythm, as Friel's stage directions make clear, is too frantic for pure joy: 'But the movements seem caricatured; and the sound is too loud; and the beat is too fast... With this too loud music, this shouting — calling — singing, this parodic reel, there is a sense of order being consciously subverted, of the women consciously and crudely caricaturing themselves, indeed of near hysteria being induced.' In *Riverdance's* too loud music and too fast beat, there was, also, an element of hysteria and self-caricature, the shadow both of Catholic puritanism at home and of Stage Irish display abroad. Both were present, not on stage, but in the wings, as alternative possibilities of failure, the monster and the whirlpool between which *Riverdance* had to trip the light fantastic. Its grace was that of an elegant swerve away from dangerous traps. The feeling of release was in direct proportion to the repression from which it sprang.

The pleasure of *Riverdance* was unimaginable without the pain of emigration. Its choreographer and original principal dancers were children of the Irish immigrants in big American cities. Its narrative was about emigration itself — a dance developed on a small, misty island having to find its feet on the streets of New York, amongst a plethora of competing cultures. And its cultural form — Irish traditional music and dance re-figured as a big Broadway show — had the tangled relationship between Ireland and America embedded within it. Its raptures could not be entirely careless.

There is, in Ireland, a deep connection between dancing and displacement. In most cultures, dancing is an expression of the community, a ritual of togetherness. To go to a dance is to participate in a place. Through dancing, the private — sexual desire, courtship, family relationships — is played out as a public display. The gap between the personal and the social is narrowed. But in Ireland, for most of the 20th century at least, dancing was often about avoiding the community, even of avoiding communication. It became a private activity, an act, not of communication or expression, but of escape.

In his *Limerick Rural Survey* of 1962, the most detailed and brilliant description of the Irish countryside before the radical changes brought by multinational industry and membership of the EEC, Patrick McNabb notes that, even those young people who stayed at home preferred to dance outside their own townland or parish:

'Most young people preferred to dance outside their own immediate neighbourhood. Whenever possible they did not support the local halls. Boys in particular, who have a car at their disposal, think nothing of travelling long distances to dances, and of visiting three or four different halls in one night. A better band, floor, better dancers, greater selection of partners were mentioned as reasons for going further afield to dance. But further questioning showed that the home dance hall could compete with others and that people from outside the area came to dance in local halls. When the contradiction in their statements was shown, boys and girls then gave the explanation that 'you could let your hair down' in outside halls. Since for the most part those people are well behaved at dances, 'letting down one's hair' does not mean rowdiness but simply escaping the observation of the home community... Dancing is as anonymous in rural areas as it is in cities. Conversation is pared down to laconic statements about the floor, the band or the weather.'

It was precisely this connection between mobility and dancing that most alarmed the Catholic Church in the early years of the Irish State. In a pastoral letter issued in 1931, Cardinal MacRory pointed out the moral danger posed by the willingness of young people to travel long distances to dances: 'Even the present travelling facilities make a difference. By bicycle, motor car and bus, boys and girls can now travel great distances to dances, with the result that a dance may now be attended by unsuitables from a distance.'

As a form, Irish Dancing (as opposed to dancing in Ireland — the two were emphatically not the same thing) had been constructed as a defence against distant unsuitables by excluding glamour, seduction, sexual display, urbanity, modernity, all that was immodest or indecent, from the way people danced. In a pastoral letter of 1924, for instance, Cardinal Logue distinguished Irish dancing from modern dancing: 'it is no small commendation of Irish dances that they cannot be danced for long hours. That, however, is not their chief merit. And while it is not part of our business to condemn any decent dance, Irish dances are not to be put out of the place that is their due in any educational establishment under our care. They may not be the fashion in London and Paris. They should be the fashion in Ireland. Irish dances do not make degenerates.' Conversely, of course, dances that did make degenerates were, by definition, not Irish.

In his 1996 book, *Last Night's Fun*, the Belfast poet and traditional musician Ciaran Carson defines the *ceili* of his teens as 'a social event imprimatured by the Catholic Church where boys and girls met each other under close sacerdotal supervision and practised minimal-contact dancing'. In that sense, all Irish Dancing was liturgical. It was an act of piety, a homage to the holy trinity of Catholicism, Irish nationalism and sexual continence.

An unsupervised dance was not an Irish Dance. One of Fianna Fail's first pieces of social legislation was The Public Dance Halls Act of 1935, requiring all dances to be licensed and to operate under strict supervision. The priests and the police used the legislation to break up dances at crossroads and in houses, the places where a living, non-commercial tradition of dancing survived. Breandan Breathnach, the historian of Irish traditional music and dancing, said of the 1935 Public Dancehalls Act that 'Whether it was intended or not, when the Act was introduced, it was applied to ordinary houses, and there isn't any doubt in my mind that there were places in the country where there was a kind of collusion between the Guard and the Parish priest, for ordinary dances, where there was no question of people paying. I have found people say in Connemara who were frightened to have a dance. The Act was misused and misdirected against ordinary houses.'

The County Clare fiddle player Junior Crehan told an RTE radio documentary in the 1980s that 'We were forbidden to have a dance. The Guards were sent out. I was at a couple of them where the Guards came out and took names and the owner of the house was brought to court and fined, and the poor man was only trying to make a few pounds to pay the rent or the rates... The dancehalls started then.'

According to Crehan, there was an intimate connection between the death of dancing and emigration: "The country house dance was gone, and the country man didn't fit in with the jazz and the foxtrot, so it died away. And a world of fellas left for England. They had no social activity at all, nothing here for them, and they got fed up, so they went off. There was no country house dance after that then. Except you'd have a small party if Americans came, and friends would be invited. It wouldn't be like the old times at all."

And yet there was also an intimate connection between emigration and the survival of Irish dancing as an element of American popular culture. Watching Jimmy Cagney play George M. Cohan in *Yankee Doodle Dandy*, I always assumed that the original Broadway song-and-dance man was a Jew called Cohen. The knowledge that he was actually a Mick called Keohane given to proclaiming that

Proud of all the Irish blood that's in me,
Divil a man can say a word agin me.

brought with it the delightful but slightly disturbing realisation that there was a real connection between *Round the House and Mind the Dresser* and the soft shoe shuffle. Cohan's father Jerry, himself the son of Famine immigrants, was a famous traditional Irish dancer, who developed new versions of jigs and reels for the travelling variety show in which his son first appeared on stage, dancing to Irish tunes played by the great uilleann piper Patsy Touhey. Suddenly, all our memories of wincing as we tried to dance *The Walls of Limerick* brick by brick had to be seen in a different light. The idea that there might be a link between ceilis and chorus lines was hard to get your head around. *Riverdance* took that odd connection and reworked into the most unlikely reconciliation of Irish piety and American pizzaz since Annie Murphy fell in love with Eamon Casey, except that *Riverdance* went on to live happily ever after.

It became customary to talk of *Riverdance* as an act of reclamation, a taking-back for popular entertainment of a form that had been prettified and stultified. And such talk was accurate enough as far as it went. But what was most significant was that what was being reclaimed was not just Irish folk dancing, but also the Irish contribution to the Broadway musical. The tradition that was being revived was not that of de Valera's comely maidens dancing at the crossroads but that of George M. Cohan. *Yankee Doodle Dandy* was taking its place with *The Walls of Limerick* or *The Mason's Apron* as an authentic antecedent for contemporary Irish culture. In that sense, *Riverdance* was as much a re-definition as a reclamation of Irish tradition.

To get a sense of just how unlikely the cultural logic of *Riverdance* really is, you have to remember that it was, in racing parlance, by The Eurovision Song Contest out of James Flannery's production of W.B. Yeats's *Cuchulain Cycle* at the Abbey Theatre in 1989. It began life as the interval act at the Eurovision, but actually contradicted the very notion of Ireland as a European country, placing it instead firmly in an American context. It took a form of dance that had seemed to be part of the dead world of Irish cultural nationalism and re-made it, while at the same time bringing it closer to what it had originally been, putting back the missing ingredient of sex that had been distilled out of Irish dance by a mixture of Victorian piety, nationalist purity and Catholic suspicion of the body.

The Yeats connnection was at once entirely surprising and fairly obvious. Jim Flannery, who is, like the original principle dancers in *Riverdance*, Michael Flatley and Jean Butler, a second generation Irish-American, brought together Bill Whelan's music, Davy Spillane's pipes and whistles, Noel Eccles's percussion, serious choral work, theatrical choreography, and more than a touch of American showbiz populism in his staging of the Cuchulain plays at the Peacock in 1989. No one could have expected the outcome of all this to be anything like *Riverdance*, and of course without the addition of Michael Flatley's brilliant re-invention of Irish step dancing and of Michael McGlynn's Anuna choir, it would not have been. Nevertheless it is a striking indicator of cultural *chutzpah* that a spectacular piece of 1990s Irish showbiz like *Riverdance* owes as many regards to W.B. Yeats as it does to Broadway. It is as if Spanish culture had suddenly thrown up a popular spectacle that drew in equal measure from Julio Iglesias, flamenco and Federico Garcia Lorca. *Riverdance* suggests that Irish popular culture is now so adaptable that it can put together almost any number of contradictory influences and elements.

The show's combination of Celtic twilight and Broadway starlight is perhaps not as strange as it might seem, though. After all, Yeats's idea of a theatre which would combine drama, dance and music had more in common with the American musical than the old distinction between modernist high art and vulgar entertainment could ever envisage. And, on the other side, as George M. Cohan's re-working of his Irish roots reminds us, vaudeville song-and-dance had more than a touch of Celtic twilight in its promiscuous make-up. Whelan, Flatley, Butler and producer Moya Doherty recognised just how radically the old high art/low art distinction has been exploded in contemporary culture, and just how free you are in Ireland now to pick up the shattered pieces and glue them together in any combination you like.

Yet that freedom itself is a legacy of emigration. For in both its conflation of high art and low art, and its voracious cultural promiscuity, *Riverdance* recaptured a mix of elements very like the staple Irish music and dance culture of New York 40 years before. In the 1950s and 1960s, the United Irish Counties Association held an annual Feis which Rebecca S. Miller has described as follows: 'the Feis sought to equate folk arts with high arts. In some instances, the required pieces for the instrumental competitions were classical selections in addition to classical arrangements of Irish tunes. Maureen Glynn Connolly, a fiddler and pianist born in Brooklyn in 1950, remembers learning pieces by Bach as well as arranged Irish tunes to compete at the Feis in the late 1950s and early 1960s... the Feis attempted to legitimize the practice of Irish traditional culture in a modern urban context.'

Miller has also described the typical repertoire at the main New York Irish dancehall, the City Centre in Manhattan, in the 1950s, where Brendan Ward's All Star Orchestra was the resident band: 'On a typical weekend evening, Brendan Ward's orchestra played the popular American dance standards and Ward's unique Americanised Irish songs... With continental and Latin music also in demand, Ward led his 12-piece orchestra through Strauss waltzes, rumbas, cha-chas, and tangos. After a 40-minute set, the big band would take a break and an accordionist, pianist and drummer would take the stage and play a 20-minute set of old-time Irish waltzes, an occasional continental waltz such as *The Blue Danube* and popular Irish songs. After Brendan Walsh's orchestra returned for another 40-minute set, the Irish accordionist would follow with 20 more minutes of *ceili* dance music —

traditional set-pieces, jigs, and reels, depending on the dance.'

What made *Riverdance* so exhilirating was the sense, not so much of invention as of recognition. The slickness, the confidence and the professionalism may have been a far cry from the immigrant dancehalls of the 1950s, and the elements may have been intertwined rather than being presented in sequence, but the cultural mix was the same. Ireland and America, folk art and Tin Pan Alley, tangos and reels, the pure and the hybrid, have never been, for most people most of the time, distinct entities.

And yet, *Riverdance* could not have worked without an underlying respect for Irish traditional music and dance, without its implicit acknowledgement that folk culture has a life, and a truth of its own, and that while it can be adapated in any number of ways, it does not exist merely in order to be adapted. *Riverdance* turned its brazen cheek both ways. On the one hand, the American side of Michael Flatley — the utterly unapologetic show-off who has, it must be admitted, nothing to be modest about — was given free rein, and the show was almost naive in its lack of embarrassment about putting on the glitz. But if it was naked and unashamed in its willingness to risk kitsch, it was equally so in its belief that unadorned traditional music could be placed side-by-side with showbiz razmatazz. It kept its nerve just as much for Davy Spillane playing *Caoineadh Cu Chulainn* on the uileann pipes or for Aine Ui Cheallaigh's exquisite singing of *A Chumaraigh Aoibhinn* as for its big, Broadway-style chorus lines.

Oddly enough, given its antecedents in the Yeats Festival, the one thing the show didn't have was dramatic coherence. Its second half in particular, with its gospel singers and tap, flamenco and Russian dancers became a series of star turns rather than a coherent whole. The narrative point — that Irish culture has taken its place in the international melting pot — was illustrated rather than fully realised. And this was an important falling short for, unlike most dance shows, *Riverdance* drew its energy as much from what it was saying as from what it did. What made it more than an international showbusiness product was the way it liberated locked-up elements of Irish tradition, the way it became, quite self-consciously, a parable of the modernisation of Irish culture.

The importance of that parabolic element in the show, and the delicacy of its cultural filigree, was made much more obvious by the awfulness of its illegitimate offspring, Michael Flatley's *Lord of the Dance*. Seldom in the history of dance can the sublime and the ridiculous have been in such close step as in Flatley's extravaganza, staged after his acrimonious split from the *Riverdance* company. Liberated from the constraints of working with formidable collaborators in *Riverdance*, the prancing Puck was free to do both his best and his worst. The mesmerising physical power of this embodied whirlwind was on full and unabashed display. So, alas, were crass egomania and the cultural idiocy that can result when a knowing post-modern Irishness tips over into the packaged, de-politicised, de-contextualised Celticism that has become such an attractive way of selling Ireland-without-tears.

There is no doubt that Michael Flatley is a kind of genius. As a choreographer, his combination of Irish step dancing with tap and flamenco is genuinely original. As a cultural entrepreneur, he has put a dizzying spin on the old story of Ireland and America. And as a dancer, he storms the walls of scepticism by sheer force of physical virtuosity and takes control of the viewer's senses.

Lord of the Dance was largely about declaring this genius, and therein lay both its sporadic magnificence and its persistent awfulness. After *Riverdance*, Flatley seemed to feel that he had everything to prove. Not only was the choreography of *Riverdance* released into full flood — more thunderous chorus lines, more insistent hard-shoe hammerings, more noise — but it was also much more brazenly in thrall to the star turn. In both senses of the term, Michael Flatley was making a show of himself.

To some extent, of course, Flatley can justify his overweening egotism. The dancing, not just from Flatley but also from his principal partners, was often superb. But its power seemed always to be fuelled by testosterone. There were essentially two modes. One, the mostly male hard-shoe macho drive, where speed, sound and muscular tension combined into a successful if coercive spectacle. The other, the mostly female soft-shoe gambolling, was often, especially in the chorus work, unbearably fey. The *Lord* worked best in masculine ways.

This would be relatively unproblematic were it not reinforced at every turn by the storyline. The plot, such as it was, was a ludicrous concoction of cod-Celtic mysticism, *West Side Story* and *Star Wars* in which Michael Flatley, defends his Clan of the Celts, struggles with Don Dorcha (aka Darth Vader), the Dark Lord, avoids the siren call of the Morrighan and wins the heart of Saoirse, the Irish Colleen. It reached breathtaking heights of absurdity towards the end, when Flatley's macho posturing, unchecked by any semblance of irony or humour, was trapped out with stage tricks that would embarrass Ming the Merciless.

To this extent, *Lord of the Dance* was merely risible. But Ronan Hardiman's music and what it did to Irish folk culture was no laughing matter. At one level, its immediate effect was to remind us of just how critical Bill Whelan's music was to the success of *Riverdance*. But at another, it underpinned a bare-faced vulgarity that was truly ugly.

The moments of unadorned Irish traditional music in *Riverdance* defined the cultural space in which the whole show operated. The elements of kitsch and of Broadway pizazz took their place in a genuine relationship between tradition and modern popular culture. In *Lord of the Dance*, on the other hand, the relationship to Gaelic culture was strictly smash-and-grab. It was not just that there wasn't a single musical moment that was other than shallow and meretricious. It was that there were several moments of almost unprecedented philistinism. The worst of them came near the end of the first act when 'Erin the Goddess' dressed in a flowing green get-up sang *Anach Cuain*.

This is a great *sean nós song*, an unutterably dignified lament for those who died in a mass-drowning in Lough Corrib. It is, in a real sense, a piece of sacred art, committing to immortal memory the grief of a community. In Flatley's show, it was sung entirely without sympathy, without context and without meaning. Its words were treated as so much suitably high-sounding gibberish, its air as a useful slab of Celticy sound. No reference at all was made to the content of the song: its title wasn't even printed in the programme.

As an act of cultural vandalism, this was the musical equivalent of kicking over the headstones in a cemetery. As a crass appropriation of other people's grief it rivalled in obtuseness and obscenity the French synchronised swimming team which planned to perform a routine on the theme of the Holocaust in the Atlanta Olympics. Cultural imperialism is a much abused term, but when, as here, an entire culture is much abused, it seemed appropriate. In *Riverdance*, Michael Flatley was having a ball with elements of traditional Irish culture. Here, wrapped in the magic cloak of his own self-regard, he seemed content to dance on its grave.

What *Lord of the Dance* showed is how easy it is for Irish culture, in its adaptation to a global, commodified entertainment business, to teeter over the edge of boldness and into an abyss of banality, to mistake liberation from a repressive past for crass ignorance of the collective memory locked up in traditional forms, to lose the core of awkwardness and resistance without which any piece of art must be either insipid or destructive.

At the very core of Irish dance music is a tension between the familiar and the strange, the social and the individual, home and away. The composer Sean O Riada defined it (in *Our Musical Heritage*) in terms of days. Every day is the same in that the sun rises and sets. But within that immutable form, days contain an infinite variety of possibilities: 'Every day possesses the same basic characteristics, follows the same fundamental pattern, while at the same time each day differs from the last in its ornamentation of events.'

So it is with Irish dance music. The basic form is circular, repetitive and predictable. It expresses a sense of life as being fixed and stable, of a community containing within itself all that needs to be known or experienced. It is, in other words, traditional. But the pleasure of the music lies in the play of improvisation and ornamentation against this basic form. Trills and grace-notes, careful disorderings of the tune, swoops and soarings, are the ornamentations that reflect the unpredictability of events. The permanent and the contingent, tradition and change, the settled and the mobile, place and displacement — each is, in the texture of the music, as necessary as the other. To keep its feet in a global culture, never mind to dance to its incessant rhythms, Ireland needs precisely such a balance.

Setting Foot On Arch Hill

In his memoir of growing up in the small West Virginia town of Piedmont, the black American writer Henry Louis Gates Jnr, remembers that the whole west side of the place, where the road rises towards the Allegheny Mountains, was called 'Arch Hill': 'I figured that it was called that because it was shaped like the arch of your foot. Twenty five years later, I learned that what the coloured people called 'Arch Hill' had all along been 'Irish Hill'. Cracked me up when Pop told me that.'

The trick of the tongue that turned Irish into Arch, transforming the ethnic identity of the O'Rourkes, O'Briens, O'Reillys and O'Neills who lived there into a human footprint was a happy one. To hear in the word 'Irish' the shape of a foot in motion is to catch the true note of a culture that is not just marked but actually defined by the perpetual motion of the people who bear it. Emigration and exile, the journeys to and from home, are the very heartbeat of Irish culture. To imagine Ireland is to imagine a journey.

The nature of that journey has changed, however. What used to be a voyage beyond the point of no return is now, increasingly, a series of temporary shifts. The symbol of permanent Irish emigration is no longer the wake but the wedding. The American Wake that used to mark the sense of passing to 'the other side' has been replaced by the wedding, for it is only through marrying abroad that young Irish people now declare themselves as immigrants rather than emigrants. But weddings are always more contingent than wakes. They have no finality, no certainty. They are a declaration of intent rather than a statement of immutable fact.

One way of envisaging that change is through the familiar metaphor of margin and centre. It can be said with some confidence that historic Irish emigration marked a movement from the margin to the centre, in the sense that rural Irish migrants moved from a largely pre-modern society to a modern one. The shift in space could also be construed as a shift in time, or more accurately in period. The emigrant going from West Mayo to the Lower East Side in the 1850s was stepping into the future, moving not just to another continent, but to another era. But in the late 20th century, the metaphor of margin and centre no longer works.

For one thing, it is a metaphor appropriate to a flat earth, and the earth is no longer, in cultural or economic terms, flat. It has become global, an increasingly integrated system that is, if not quite de-centred, at least multi-centred. Since the centre is no longer capable of being expressed in simple geographical terms, moving from one part of the globe to another no longer necessarily implies a shift from margin to centre. The nature of the transition depends much more critically on the place of the emigrant within the home society. Some Irish emigrants (for example, a computer graduate who moves from IBM in Dublin to Wall Street) are already economically, psychologically, and to a large degree culturally, a part of the centre before they leave.

Nor is the nature of marginality unchanged. The long process whereby cultures of the centre have romanticised certain cultures of the margin has itself altered the meaning of those cultures. There is now a zone, at once cultural and geographical, that belongs neither to margin nor centre, and much of Ireland belongs in it. The Australian poet Les Murray has argued that the true margin now is not on the outer edge but in the middle. It lies between the metropolitan centre on the one side and what Murray calls the *meta-margin* on the other. This latter zone is 'the exotic, the wilderness, the vanishing archaic'. And certain aspects of Irish culture — those that were truly marginal for most of the nineteenth century — now belong clearly to the meta-margin. Tourism has completed and commodified the process that Romanticism and Celticism started in the last century. It has made the exotic and archaic aspects of Irish culture not merely acceptable to but desirable for the centre. And this in turn has had tangible effects for Irish emigrants, particularly those going to America, where Irish emigration has been favoured by visa programmes over emigration from more truly marginal societies.

To understand this change, it is necessary first to understand just how central emigration has been to the way Ireland understands itself. In Liam O'Flaherty's stark, grief-stricken story, *Going Into Exile,* for instance, you can feel how the ebbing away of human reality in the act of emigration opens up a blank space to be filled by the imagination. There is an American Wake in progress, marking the move to Boston the following day of a son and a daughter, Michael and Mary. O'Flaherty writes it like the Last Supper, a feast that is also a sombre preparation for a death. As the morning of departure dawns, the unseen, the unreal, the imagined takes a subtle grip:

'The stars were growing dim. A long way off invisible sparrows were chirping in their ivied perch in some distant hill or other... Cocks crew, blackbirds carolled, a dog let loose from a cabin by an early riser chased madly after an imaginary robber, barking as if his tail were on fire. The people said goodbye and began to stream forth from Feeney's cabin.'

Eventually, at the end of the story, the mother is left in a world of desolate imaginings, 'listening foolishly for an answering cry', imagining she can 'hear the crags simmering under the hot rays of the sun. It was something in her head that was singing.' This counterpoint between an emptying house and the tightening grip of the imaginary (the invisible sparrow, the imaginary robber, the simmering crags, the singing in the head) is emblematic of modern Irish culture. Reading between the lines, discerning meaning in the empty spaces, is often the task in hand.

A later O'Flaherty story, *The Letter,* virtually a follow-up to *Going Into Exile*, can stand as a metaphor for this task. A peasant family is working in the fields. Their eldest daughter Mary has gone to America. They have had no letter from her for a long time, though a neighbour has written to say that Mary is without work. The family's two youngest daughters arrive home from school with a letter they have received from the postman. It is from Mary. The father opens it and takes out a check for £20, enough to buy a new horse to replace the one that died a year before. There is unbounded joy. Then the eldest son reads the letter aloud.

"'Dear Parents', the son began. 'Oh mother, I am so lonely.' It's all covered with blots same as if she were crying on the paper. 'Daddy why did I... why did I ever... ever...' It's hard to make it out... yes... 'why did I ever come to this awful place? Say a prayer for me every night, mother. Your loving daughter Mary.'"

After a long silence, the whole family begins to wail and weep. Nothing has been said, nothing made explicit. There is no explanation for the £20 check or for the daughter's anguish. But the family fills in the blanks. Reading between the lines and making out the tear-blotched letters, they imagine an unthinkable truth. Their reading of the letter is also a kind of writing, an engagement of their creative imaginations that gives shape and meaning to the barely discernible realities that the letters on the page hint at. This is what a culture defined by emigration does — it writes itself as it reads itself.

There is, of course, a profound connection for all cultures between nationality and the fictive imagination. All national borders are, at a fundamental level, works of fiction. They separate the nation from all that is not the nation. And what they enclose is not just a physical space, but also an imaginative one. Nations are the product of history rather than geography, of culture rather than race. Like a book or a play, they are made up. 'The nation', as Peter Stallybrass puts it, 'has to be invented or written; and written, what is more, in the crucial and troubling knowledge that it could be written otherwise. It is *because* the nation could be written otherwise that the act of writing must be forgotten, transformed instead into the act of reading a pre-given past.'

The conflict between writing the nation and reading it lies at the heart of Irish culture in the 20th century. It is an insoluble conflict because it arises from the most difficult contradiction of Irish politics and economics — the contradiction between place and people, between the search for a fixed national space and the existence of an unfixed, mobile population, between a stable definition of Irishness and the unstable ambiguities that elude it.

The geographical Ireland, the bounded island, is a place that can be read. It can be imagined, albeit problematically, as the result of a given past, as the present form of an innate and immemorial Irishness. The second, demographic Ireland is a nation that cannot be read but must be written. And because it must be written, it could be written otherwise. Existing, as it does, imaginatively, it is always open to the possibility of being re-imagined. As such, it poses a constant threat to the first Ireland. It questions its readings by remembering that they, too, were once written, that they are inventions, that they represent, not an innate expression of the nation, but merely the one strand from a range of possibilities that happened to develop within the frame of the island of Ireland.

The great German critic Walter Benjamin, in his essay *The Storyteller* reminds us that there are two kinds of storytellers, embodied, respectively, in the tiller of the soil and the trading seaman. The first carries 'the lore of the past, as it best reveals itself to natives of a place.' The second is imbued with 'the lore of faraway places, such as a much-travelled man brings home.' Storytelling, Benjamin says, is most potent when it comes from 'the most intimate interpenetration of these two archaic types.' Sometimes, at its most powerful — as in for instance the work of James Joyce — Irish culture combines the lore of the past and the lore of faraway places. But more often the two have been in contest with each other.

Modern Irish writing comes out of the attempt of the Irish Literary Revival to posit Ireland as a culture that could be read, and read through the lore of the past. The whole idea of a revival presupposes a belief that there is some intact inheritance from the past which can be recovered by careful reading. By clearing away the false impositions of Britishness and urban modernity, the lines of a culture implicit in the island itself could be deciphered and their meaning restored. Thus, W. B. Yeats, for instance, claimed that the modern Irish drama would be founded on a mediaeval poetic, and that he could track any authentic folk expression still in use back to classical times.

This was, of course, untrue. The Revival was a writing that pretended to be a reading, an act of invention that pretended to be an act of restoration. The fact of emigration, the fact that the immediate past of the Revival period was one of extraordinary dispersion, was glossed over in the Revival's emphasis on the authenticity of place. By taking place rather than people as the touchstone of Irishness, the Revival was able to appeal to a sense of continuity and stability that were simply unavailable in contemporary Irish experience. But this effort involved an inevitable strain.

The worries in the early Abbey Theatre over Lady Gregory's play *Twenty Five*, for instance, give the game away. The play was originally to be called *Fifty*, referring to the number of pounds the hero Christie brings home after two years in America. The Fay brothers who ran the acting company originally rejected the play on the basis that if young men were shown that they could save £50 in two years, they would all be off to America. Lady Gregory had to re-write it, cutting the sum in half and changing the title to *Twenty Five*. Emigration undercut the very notion that an Irish theatre could safely reflect Irish reality.

Even more emblematic of the contradictions, and more revealing of the fault-lines, is a paragraph in Padraic O Conaire's novel *Deoraiocht (Exile)* published in 1910 as the first major novel in the Gaelic language. It is striking in itself that one of the first real literary expressions of the language revival centres, not on the recovery of a fixed place and a finished past, but on the tormented wanderings in Ireland and England of a displaced man who becomes a freak in a travelling circus. Even more striking, though, is the irony of the following passage, describing social gatherings in a part of London called Little Ireland, inhabited mostly by people from Munster:

"There would be a man there who could relate the contents of Keating's *History of Ireland* as well as a man who knew nothing about it. And if somebody were to disagree with anything the *savant* said, he would just go to the big trunk he had brought with him from Ireland and take out a parcel wrapped in linen. He would open the parcel and take out a large book in manuscript. And how careful he was of that book! He would then show you in black and white where you had been wrong. And when he closed the book to put it away he would look at you as if to say. 'Now what have you to say for yourself?' But he never said a word."

O Conaire's image of this man with his linen-wrapped parcel of unarguable history brought from Ireland into exile is a perfect example of the act of writing being forgotten, and transformed instead into the act of reading a pre-given past. The struggle to survive in England is occluded by the struggle to hang on to a fixed, finished identity. Where history and geography are confused and displaced by emigration, the appeal to the authority of an invented past becomes coercive. In the Little Irelands of the Irish diaspora, there was for a long time an overwhelming temptation to read Ireland as a closed book rather than to imagine it as a blank page waiting to be written.

Irish emigrants were removed, not merely from Ireland to elsewhere, but from the land to the city. And their absence from the landscape is what makes it possible for them to disappear from the emergent culture of modern Ireland. That invention of modern Ireland was driven by the Romantic search for a culture organically rooted in an authentic landscape. What was to be read in that cultural quest was the landscape itself. John Montague, in *The Rough Field* imagines

The whole landscape a manuscript
We had lost the skill to read

and the image could stand as a summation of the nationalist project, and its desire to regain the skill to scrutinise the landscape until it gave up its hidden, authentic meanings.

But emigrants were not merely, by definition, absent from this landscape. They were absent from all landscape, ensconced as they were in cities. And this perverse desire to live in cities was, to many nationalist intellectuals, incomprehensible. George Russell, writing in 1912, noted the 'growing dislike of the land among the rising generation. How many Irishmen go to the land in the States? Not one in twenty, not in a hundred — hardly one in a thousand. They have been on the land in Ireland, and they go anywhere — to any crowded slum — rather than to the fields.' Forty years later, the novelist and playwright Bryan MacMahon noted that 'The pattern of Irish life in the shoddy towns of industrial England is yet to reveal itself; it seems rather a pity that the rural Irish did not emigrate to rural England.' What he does not note is that there is an innate connection between the first half of his sentence and the second: Irish life in industrial England could not 'reveal itself' in Irish culture precisely because it was not rural and therefore lay outside the dominant forms and ideologies.

This exclusion was, of course, self-perpetuating. Emigration created a vicious circle for Irish culture: the difficulty of imagining urban life robbed Irish culture of much of its capacity to embrace its emigrants; the failure to embrace emigrant experience, meanwhile, made it hard for Irish culture to develop ways of imagining urban experience. Many essential Irish stories belong, in the first instance, to other cultures. The most profound dramatisations of the Irish experience of social mobility and of the gap between parents born in poverty and children born in comfort, belong in the American theatre, in the plays of Eugene O'Neill, especially Long Day's Journey into Night. The most coherent narrative of Irish Catholic working class life — James T. Farrell's *Studs Lonergan* novels — belongs to American fiction. The most troubling exploration of the Irish as both colonised and, in the context of the genocide of Native Americans, colonisers, — John Ford's film *The Searchers* — belongs to American cinema. Emigration simplified the representations of Irish experience and made it possible to imagine Ireland as a cultural monolith.

Where culture is understood as immanent in place, as it is in the Irish revival, the displaced emigrant can disappear from the culture, can suffer an almost literal loss of voice. Again, John Montague, born in Brooklyn but brought back to Ireland at the age of four, gets to the heart of the matter. In his poem *A Flowering Absence* he recalls his experience of emigration and return as a loss of language itself, his childhood self taunted by a schoolmistress 'who hunted me publicly down/ to near speechlessness':

> *Where did he get that outlandish accent?*
> *What do you expect, with no parents,*
> *sent back from some American slum:*
> *none of you are to speak like him!*

The effect, he writes, was that 'I could no longer utter/ those magical words I had begun/ to love...'

In the silence left by emigration, the aesthetics of emptiness took hold. Empty wilderness is seen as innately more noble than ordinary urban existence. George Russell is explicit in his contempt for Irish towns, which he describes, significantly, as 'excresences on the face of nature':

'Our small Irish country towns, in their external characteristics, are so arid and unlovely that one longs for a lodge in some vast wilderness as a relief from the unbearable meanness. Better look out on boundless sand and boundless sky, on two immensities, than on these mean and straggling towns, those disreputable public houses, those uncleansed footways like miry manure yards.'

Michael Collins also objects to urban life on aesthetic grounds, remarking that 'the fine, splendid surface of Ireland is besmirched by our towns and villages — hideous medleys of contemptible dwellings and mean shops and squalid public houses, not as they should be in material fitness, the beautiful human expressions of what our God-given country is!' And Collins, too, looks to the deserted places — in his case Achill, a beautiful landscape made all the more beautiful by mass emigration — for the idealised contrast to squalid urban life.

As a way of filling up the space left by departing emigrants, and at the same time of reading Ireland so as to elide the awkward emigrant experience, this kind of nationalist Romanticism was very potent. It is worth noting in passing that even the most heart-wrenching and immediate reminder of emigration — the ruined villages and cottages that still litter the countryside — may not necessarily have been read by Irish Romanticism as images of defeat and despair. Luke Gibbons has noted, suggestively, that the dominance of ruins — particularly of round towers — in Irish nationalist iconography marked the special set of associations which ruins evoked:

'The very survival of ruins meant that they had withstood the ravages of time and successive waves of invasion, thus attesting to the continuity between past and present and the resilience of Gaelic civilisation. It was this which fastened the link between ruin and political violence, for the affirmation of an ancient separate civilisation meant that a complete break with Britain was required, outside the limited confines of parliamentary reform.'

There is a connection between the contempt for ordinary urban buildings expressed by Michael Collins and the IRA's subsequent willingness to destroy Irish cities. George Russell makes it when, just after the passage about sand and sky quoted above, he remarks that 'For if one has a soul and any love for beauty he must feel like an anarchist if he strays into an Irish country town, and must long for bombs to wreck and dynamite to obliterate.' In this obscure sense, the process of cultural obliteration of emigrants and the campaign of violence which established the Irish state itself are connected through the image of dereliction. As one of the most self-conscious of exiles, Samuel Beckett, noted acerbically 'What constitutes the charm of our country, apart, of course from its scant population, and this without the help of the meanest contraceptive, is that all is derelict, with the sole exception of history's ancient faeces.'

Daniel Corkery, the former IRA man who was the most coherent ideologue of Irish cultural nationalism, makes the obliteration most explicit. In *Synge and Anglo-Irish Literature,* he begins his argument by first winnowing out most of the best-known living Irish writers, among them Padraic Colum, Thomas McGreevy, Austin Clarke, James Joyce, James Stephens, Sean O'Casey, Liam O'Flaherty, George Moore and Bernard Shaw. Noting that all of them live outside Ireland, he performs a rhetorical sleight-of-hand in which they all disappear as Irish writers:

'Now unless one can show that the demands of the alien market are on all fours with the demands of the home market, how can this literature be Anglo-Irish? How can it be a national literature? The question is not: Can expatriates produce national literature? but: Can expatriates writing for an alien market produce national literature?'

The question, of course, is rhetorical, for it is entirely clear that, to Corkery, expatriates cannot produce a national literature. Note how beautifully circular this argument is. At least in part because of censorship, which Corkery does not mention, there is no home market. Because there is no home market, the writers must go abroad and write for foreign audiences. Because they write for foreign audiences, they are not Irish writers. Because they are not Irish writers, why should anyone worry if their books are banned?

In Corkery's ideology of the indigenous and the alien, which is classically nationalist in its concern with fixed opposites, its paradoxical obsession with England which can only imagine Ireland as not-England, the Abbey Theatre itself may be, as he puts it, 'no more than an exotic branch of English literature'. Since there is, in his mind, no real Irish writing or Irish theatre in the English language at all, then nothing that happens within it can have any significance. This is something much more profound than censorship — it is obliteration. The point is not so much to control and to shape the work of writers as to make it disappear by constructing an ideological frame within which that work is almost literally unthinkable.

Not the least of the ironies of this willed obliteration of the vast bulk of Irish literary achievement on the grounds that it was produced abroad is that most of the realist tradition in Irish culture is the creation of exiles. The dominance of Romanticism in Irish culture meant that the realist project of Frank O'Connor and Sean O'Faolain, who for the most part stayed in Ireland, was doomed. The would-be writer Michael Dempsey in Brinsley MacNamara's novel *The Clanking of Chains* is more or less forced into exile. MacNamara notes that 'He would have to be a realist dealing only with facts in whatever country he might go to, and it is part of the irony of things that he could not be this same realist in his own country.'

Realism in writing is a concern with the bits and pieces of experience rather than with a grand, archetypal narrative. In writers of the diaspora like James Hanley, who doesn't appear in Hogan's *Dictionary of Irish Literature,* let alone the *Field Day Anthology of Irish Writing*, a coherent narrative itself comes to seem impossible. Towards the end of Hanley's three-novel saga of an Irish family in Liverpool, *The Furys,* Peter Fury discovers that he cannot re-assemble in memory the broken pieces of his family history:

'There are so many bloody fragments that you couldn't even begin to gather them up, you couldn't even begin to think about it, and he seemed to see them fall, one after another, the members of the family to which he had once belonged. He even heard each separate thud. I wouldn't even know where to begin if I thought it was worth beginning.'

That kind of fragmented, embattled history is what emerges in the work of exiled writers. The divisions that are suppressed at home — especially the divisions of class — emerge in full voice in the work of writers like Patrick MacGill, the Irish equivalent of Zola, and Robert Noonan

(Robert Tressell), whose great work *The Ragged Trousered Philantropists* owes infinitely more to Dickens and British socialism than to Yeats and Synge. In MacGill's work, there is always the open road, in Hanley's the open sea. MacGill, in particular, manages to write about what are essentially nomadic people. Characters like Moleskin Joe in the novel of the same name and in *Children of the Dead End* belong to no fixed abode. They are part of what MacGill calls 'the migratory peoples of the road'.

And equally their stories are unstable and polymorphous. Like the autobiography of Liam O'Flaherty, the most travelled of major Irish writers, which begins with a declaration that 'Man is a born liar.', thereby undermining all claim to a single narrative truth, MacGill's novels acknowledge the instability of narrative. Against the Revival attempt to construct a fixed narrative of Ireland, the stories told about Moleskin Joe change their shape and meaning in transit. Because there is, in exile, no one place, neither is there any single narrative:

'These stories were, of course, distorted and magnified until the narrative spun in a Manchester 'model' had little semblance to the actuality which had footing in a Glasgow dosshouse.'

Such unstable stories need to be written rather than read. The remarkable thing about the exiled Irish writers, though, is how few of their stories were about exile itself. The point of departure — in Joyce's *A Portrait of the Artist as a Young Man,* for instance — is often clearly dramatised, but what happens after exile is not. Joyce most obviously conforms to John Wilson Foster's description of Irish writers taking with them 'place transformed into the memory of place and therefore transportable' in his obsessive recreations of the city he had left behind. But the description applies to many other writers. Edna O'Brien's epigraph to *A Pagan Place* — Brecht's 'I carry a brick on my shoulder in order that the world may know what my house was like'— could be placed on the title page of many Irish novels written in exile.

It is, rather, in the theatre that emigration has its most profound effect on Irish writing before the contemporary period. For it might be said that the Irish theatre in the 20th century has undergone two revivals. The first revival, that of the early Abbey, is one which keeps the reality of emigration at bay and puts itself forward as a reading of Ireland. But the second, that of the late 1950s and early 1960s, is almost entirely driven by an attempt to get to grips with emigration. Its two major playwrights, Brian Friel and Tom Murphy, are writers whose work is simply unthinkable without the continual interplay of departure and return, of home and away. In their later plays, like Friel's *Faith Healer* and Murphy's *Bailegangaire*, those concepts take on large spiritual and existential resonances, but in their early work they are literal derivations from the acutely-observed reality of emigration.

It is significant that this second revival of Irish theatre, so utterly involved with emigration, begins precisely at the point at which Irish society — in the shape of the First Programme for Economic Expansion — is at last beginning to accept the ideal of urban and industrial life. The implicit acceptance of cities in the modernisation of the Irish economy, itself a desperate response to the relentless flow of emigration in the 1950s, makes it possible for the mainstream of Irish culture to begin to comprehend the urban lives of Irish emigrants.

Tom Murphy's *A Whistle in the Dark* (1961) is set among Irish emigrants in Coventry. On the surface, it might look like an archetypal story in which Bryan MacMahon's 'pattern of Irish life in the shoddy towns of industrial England' might reveal itself. The city in which the Irishmen have placed themselves is a kind of hell, full of violence and corruption. But in fact the play turns the archetype on its head. For the move to Coventry has meant for the Carney family only an intensification of the tribal family ties and the struggle for survival in a brutish world which they knew at home in Mayo. It is not the flight from an Irish past, but actually the failure to escape that past (embodied in the monstrous shape of an archetypal patriarch, Dada) that dooms them. Emigration becomes, in Murphy's vision, a relentless exposure of Irish society at home. The import of the play is clear — emigration is not a solution to Irish problems but merely the sharpest indicator of how profound those problems are.

The same is true of the other major Irish play of the period, Brian Friel's *Philadelphia, Here I Come!* (1964), in which Gar O'Donnell's choice of staying in Donegal or emigrating to America is seen as no real choice at all, since both options are equally terrible. Friel does not set the play in America, but he does bring Irish emigres to America onto the stage, in the shape of Gar's aunt and her husband. *Philadelphia* draws its power, from the way it dramatises Ireland and America, not just as two places, but as two opposing and equally unhappy states of mind. Ireland is a place haunted by memory, America a place haunted by forgetfulness. Gar and his father are tormented by inescapable memories which may be mere inventions, showing again how emigration makes narrative unstable and untrustworthy. But Gar's American aunt is unable even to remember where she has been a few hours ago. Ireland is unbearable stasis and claustrophobia, America terrible anonymity and impermanence. One of the marks of change in the last 15 years in Ireland, however, is that this polarity is impossible in more recent Irish writing, where the feeling in O'Flaherty's *Going into Exile* that the emigrant and the Ireland left behind are two worlds as separate as death and life, has been replaced by a strong sense of Ireland itself as a place forever on the move between different worlds. In Sebastian Barry's recent play, *Prayers of Sherkin* Fanny Hawke, speaking of Sherkin Island, but touching on an image that serves for the bigger island of Ireland, asks her brother 'Do you not feel that this island is moored only lightly to the sea-bed, and might be off for the Americas at any moment?'

Such a question arises from the profound social changes in Ireland that began in the 1960s and are still in progress. The speed and scale of those changes have induced a sense of internal exile, a sense that Irish people feel less and less at home in Ireland, that Ireland has become somehow unreal. In one way or another, very many Irish people have experienced a sense of the familiar becoming unknown, unrecognisable. Ireland has become so multi-layered, so much a matter of one set of images superimposed on another, that it is hard to tell home from abroad. Thirty-five years of being an offshore economic dependency of the United States have left us with a society that is seen by an increasing number of its young people as a pale imitation of the Real Thing across the Atlantic.

The Americanisation of Ireland that began with the construction of Ireland as a European base for multinational companies has fundamentally altered the meaning of emigration itself. Since Ireland has become in some respects a little America, emigration can no longer be posited as a shift from one state of being to another. A change of location is a change of place only, and no longer a change of epoch. When Intel is making its pentium chips in the Irish countryside, Silicon Valley can hardly seem like science fiction.

For the generation of Irish writers that grew up after the First Programme of Economic Expansion, that process of alteration has also been a process of estrangement. Home has become as unfamiliar as abroad. Because Irish places have themselves been radically changed, it has been possible, in a sense, to emigrate without leaving the island. Everything begins to exist in a state of internal exile. The difference between home and abroad has shrunk to virtually nothing. Rosita Boland, for instance, looking at the moon in Australia, writes that

I was looking at a mirror image
Of a moon I had known all my life.
The points of its crescent faced the opposite way:
exactly as something does when you look at it
From the other side.

Nostalgia for a homeland has lost its meaning, not least because the images of a natural landscape that once constituted memories of home for emigrants from a predominantly rural society have been replaced by memories of a predominantly urban Irish society. What can be remembered, even from exile, is no longer a lost homeland that represents a different state of being, but a place that is of essentially the same kind as the place in which the exile now lives, all the more so because memory itself is now saturated with globalised media images.

A good example is Michael O'Loughlin's poem The Fugitive, published in 1982. The opening is conventional, evoking as it does an Irish exile in Paris, a role made stereotypical by Joyce and Beckett:

In the hour before the Metro opens
I remember you...

But the next words are not, as might be expected, 'Ireland', or 'mother', but 'Richard Kimble'. Richard Kimble was the eponymous fugitive in the American television series of the 1960s, and the exile's memory is of watching the programme as a child at home in Dublin. An exiled Irish poet's memory of home from Paris is a memory of America:

I can't remember the stories now
But in the end it's only the ikons that matter,
The silent, anonymous American city

174

With the rain running down the gutter.

For a generation that grew up on American television shows, America will always be interwoven with memories of an Irish homeland and an Irish childhood:

The muffled snarl of American accents
Coming in loud and razor sharp
Over the local interference.

This interplay of American accents and local interference is taken to its logical, and comic, conclusion in Roddy Doyle's The Commitments, where identity itself, for young working-class Dubliners is a matter of identification with American black music:

"Where are yis from? (He answered the question himself.) — Dublin. (He asked another one.) — Wha' part o' Dublin? Barrytown. Wha' class are yis? Workin' class. Are yis proud of it? Yeah, yis are. (Then a practical question.) — Who buys the most records? The workin' class. Are yis with me? (Not really.) — Your music should be abou' where you're from an' the sort o' people yeh come from. — — Say it once, say it loud, I'm black an' I'm proud. They looked at him. — James Brown."

When 'where you're from' is best expressed through the music of blacks in industrial American cities, how can you feel nostalgic for home if you're Irish and living in one of those American cities? And, furthermore, even this way of remembering is no longer distincively Irish. It is itself an aspect of a global cultural shift, of what Frederic Jameson calls 'the cultural logic of late capitalism'. Jameson remarks that, with the collapse of the high modernist ideology of style, 'the producers of culture have nowhere else to turn but to the past: the imitation of dead styles, speech through all the masks and voices stored up in the imaginary museum of a now global culture.' But the past is itself saturated with electronic imagery: it has itself become a vast collection of images, a multitudinous photographic simulacrum.' Culture — in the form of received images of, say, Richard Kimble or James Brown — becomes what nature used to be — a kind of second nature.

And if nostalgia in the old sense is impossible, so is return. The exile's dream of return has no meaning when the homeland is an ex-isle, a place forever gone. Dermot Bolger's poem and play, *The Lament for Arthur Cleary*, hark back to Eibhlin Dubh Ni Chonaill's eighteenth century *Caoineadh Art Uí Laoghaire*, in which a returned exile is killed because he no longer knows how to keep his place in a changed Ireland. Bolger's Arthur Cleary comes back to Dublin from Germany 'consumed with nostalgia/For an identity irretrievably lost':

> *But that world was dead*
> *Though you could not realise it*
> *A grey smudge of estates*
> *Charted the encroaching horizon...*

Equally, in Deirdre Madden's Remembering Light and Stone, a depressed young Irish woman in Italy visits a doctor who diagnoses 'homesickness'. She should go back, he says, to her mother. 'If I went away from my own home, what could I expect, only unhappiness and loneliness.' But she knows that this diagnosis is wrong, that the unhappiness is something she has brought with her, and that it would still await her were she to return: ' I thought that to go back to Ireland wouldn't help at all, because it was something that had been caused by my early life...' The once impossible desire to return has been replaced by a sense that returning is largely irrelevant, either because the problems are personal or because the world that was left behind has now disappeared.

Part of this process of estrangement is the alienation of the young from the images and icons of official Irish culture, now seen as repressive and exclusive. Dermot

Bolger's re-reading of Patrick Pearse in *I am Ireland,* makes this alienation explicit by speaking a variation on Patrick Pearse in the voice of an Irishwoman in exile in Birmingham:

I am Ireland
Lonelier I am than a hag on Birmingham common.

When identity is understood as being a matter of class or gender or sexual orientation before it is a matter of nationality, a sense of belonging is no longer necessarily dependent on remaining within a homeland. Indeed, the former may be incompatible with the latter.

Sometimes, of course, this sense of being at home in America or in England is a mere reflection of the bland materialism of international yuppie culture. Joe O'Connor has captured the style of the NIPPLES (New Irish Professional People Living in England):

'Well look, Dave, I took the liberty, right, I called this little chumette of mine who runs a rather interesting little unit trust outfit, who as it happens is looking for some willing hands to do a bit of cleaning at the moment, and I mentioned your name, said we were good mates, did the whole business.'

But equally this sense of being more at home in exile is often rooted in the exclusions of Irish life itself. In Emma Donohue's story, Going Back, Cyn, an Irish lesbian in London says 'Listen, I felt more of an exile for the twenty years I was in Ireland than I ever have in the twelve I've been out of it.' Conversely, many Irish people feel more culturally at home in England or America than they did in the Ireland of the 1980s, simply because those societies may be be more accomodating to their beliefs and sexual identities than the Ireland of the 1983 and 1986 referendums on abortion and divorce appeared to be.

In the new, shifting, ill-defined emigration of the 1980s, where many young Irish people found themselves in more or less constant motion, in and out of Ireland as the fluctuations of the world economy made them alternately in demand and surplus to requirements, it was no longer possible to pretend that there was a given Irish culture to be lost or held on to. And Irish writers began to reflect much more directly a sense that Ireland was a set of questions and contests rather than a given landscape waiting to be read. The relevant difference is no longer that between home and abroad, but that between the Irish themselves. Exile becomes a prism through which the diverse social forces within Ireland are separated and revealed. The Irish abroad are now written about as people divided from each other by politics, class and sexuality rather than as a single category of humanity divided from a homogenous homeland by exile.

In Michael O'Loughlin's story *Traditional Music,* for instance, Irish 'guest workers' in Germany attending a Monster Irish Folk Festival, are attacked by Germans when they throw beer cans at a man making a pro-IRA speech. The Germans think they must be English. Or in Dermot Bolger's novel *The Journey Home,* another Irish factory worker in Germany is beaten up by a fellow Irishman for supporting Turkish co-workers who go on strike.

That notion of internal exile, of an Ireland that has become, in a sense, a foreign country for many of its people, whether they stay or go, marks a profound change in the way Irish culture construes emigration. Exile is no longer a process in which a fixed identity is traded for an anonymous and impermanent one. In *True Lines*, a play devised by John Crowley in 1994, the young emigres already live in a world of anonymity and impermanence. All of its protagonists are Irish, yet the play never touches down in Ireland. Its Ireland is whatever they carry with them in four continents — the play is set in Berlin, in

Arizona, in Australia, and in Ethiopia. They travel not to escape an Ireland that is, as Gar O'Donnell's was, too numbingly continuous, but in the hope that they might find some kind of absent continuity on their journey. The play is dominated by images of being adrift in an unbounded world where random encounters and casual partings have taken the place of certainty. Its imaginative cultural reference points are the marks of human journeys across the landscape — songlines, road markings, ancient footsteps.

True Lines is the first coherent and self-conscious attempt to replace the map of a place with a map of the journies of its people but it is almost certainly the first of many. What is important is that such maps will depend on a sense of identity that is entirely imaginative, though not imaginary. The connections are not physical but cultural, matters not of a past that can be read but of a present and future that have to be constantly written and re-written. And in that writing and re-writing, the Irish abroad will have just as much of a claim on the creation of Irish culture as do the Irish at home.

Irish writers have coped with this by destroying Daniel Corkery's old ideology of the indigenous and the alien. Dermot Bolger has remarked that 'Irish writers no longer go into exile, they simply commute' and this is true metaphorically as well as literally. Their precursor, as it were, is not the James Joyce of *Ulysses*, obsessively re-creating the detail of Dublin streets from exile, but the Joyce of *Finnegans Wake,* for whom Dublin is but a template of all other places, linked linguistically to any other point on the globe. For them, as for the later Joyce, Ireland is also America and Europe. It is a linguistic, imaginative Ireland, an Ireland that cannot be read but must always be written.

In The Light of
Things as They Are:
Paul Durcan's
Ireland

I want to live with you
In the light of things as they are;
— The Dublin-Paris-Berlin-Moscow Line

One of the peculiarities of modern Irish culture is that there has been no real division between the mainstream and the avant garde. Some writers have been more conservative about form than others, but on the whole Irish writing has been remarkable for the extent to which it is impossible to divide it into a mainstream that tries to reflect social reality on the one hand and an *avant garde* that is concerned to explore the limits of form and language on the other. The reason is not hard to find: Irish reality has been, in a period of crisis and change, itself so angular and odd, so full of unlikely conjunctions and broken narratives, that a good realist has had to be also a surrealist. A jagged, many-layered reality has evoked from writers a protean, many-faced response. Paul Durcan is one of the few who have been able to immerse themselves in the flow of change and contradiction and still emerge with a coherent and distinctive body of work.

In the 1950s, when Paul Durcan was a child, the idea that Irish reality could be depicted only through the use of strange and surreal imagery suggested itself to many people. As emigration became a flood, people began to imagine Ireland as a place in which what was absent and unseen was as real as what was present and visible. A book called *The Vanishing Irish* suggested that soon there might be no one left on the island. A cartoon in *The Irish Times* showed one unsuccessful entrant in an Abbey playwrighting competition telling another: 'I suppose my dramatisation of *The Vanishing Irish* was a bit avant garde: just a set — no actors.' Equally, in 1950, the critic Thomas Hogan wrote in *Envoy* that 'among my unwritten plays there are two designed for what I thought would have been the finish up of the tradition of economic and relatively motionless acting. One is to be performed with a black curtain across the proscenium arch with holes cut in it so that the actors can shout their lines unwinkingly at the audience. The other presents possibly insuperable technical difficulties for it is designed for no actors at all.'

Before Samuel Beckett shocked European culture with theatrical images of things that were not happening, there were people in Ireland who had images in their heads of a theatre like his, not as an exercise in the *avant garde*, but as a description of reality. Irish reality itself had a surreal quality. The image of the country as a vast stage set, a cultural performance space lit by the twin glows of faith and fatherland, but with fragmented and obscure characters playing on it, seemed not like a dark absurdist fantasy, but like an only slightly exaggerated version of the real Ireland.

In *The Persian Gulf*, Paul Durcan remarks that 'Abstract Art was in Ireland long before Abstract Art.' encapsulating this strange sense in which the conditions of Irish life tended to dissolve the distinction between the real and the surreal, between the aesthetic and the political. Reading Paul Durcan is like watching a continual, picaresque play on that strange stage set that Ireland became. The stage is furnished with political and religious orthodoxies, and populated with the figures that the poet has encountered in a life that is one long journey.

In *The Only Man Never to Meet Samuel Beckett*, Durcan plays on the fact that he never met Beckett, not to distance himself from the older writer, but to emphasise an affinity much deeper than personal acquaintance. There is, in Durcan's work, no meeting with Beckett, no literary influence at work. But there is something much more striking — a continual series of random encounters with Beckett's world, encounters that are not just the usual theatrical ones, but that take place on the streets, at bus-stops, in the hustle-bustle of the city. Beckett will not leave him alone:

Whispering to him: Go away.
But he'd whisper back:
Won't go away.

The Ireland of Durcan's poems is itself so Beckettian that his meetings with Beckett are more often through life than through art. In The Beckett at the Gate, a visit to a Beckett show becomes the occasion for an erotic encounter with a young woman. In *Gogo's Late Wife Tranquilla*, we enter the extra-theatrical life of one of Beckett's best-known characters, as if Didi and Gogo were out there on the streets of Dublin.

And even when there is no explicit reference to Beckett, there are powerful echoes. It is not for nothing, for instance, that Durcan's poetic recreations of his own childhood read strikingly like one of Beckett's later novels. It is hard to read a poem like *Going Home to Mayo, Winter, 1949*, with its image of a boy and a man moving across a silent landscape in a futile journey towards death without thinking of Beckett's *Worstward Ho*. Durcan's

Thousands of crosses of loneliness planted
In the narrowing grave of the life of the father;
In the wide, wide cemetery of the boy's childhood.
feels like Beckett's old man and boy as they

Slowly with never a pause plod on and never recede.
Backs turned. Both bowed.
Joined by held holding hands.
Plod on as one. One shade. Another shade.

The point of the comparison is not to suggest a literary
influence. On the contrary, Durcan's poem was published
five years before Beckett's novel. It is the much more
interesting point that the Ireland in which Paul Durcan
writes lends itself in reality to the kind of imagery that
Beckett deployed metaphorically and metaphysically.
Beckett's abstract landscape and mute, anonymous
figures, become in some of Durcan's poems, a literal
landscape of named towns — Kilcock, Kinnegad,
Strokestown, Elphin — traversed by the poet and his
father. The abstract art that was in Ireland before abstract
art allows the poet to be at once literal and metaphysical,
at once a remembered self and a haunting figure in a dark
play of human isolation.

And indeed this is made more or less explicit in Durcan's
work. The idea that the Ireland of the 1950s is like a
Beckett play is suggested in *The Beckett at the Gate*:

Not since the Depression of the 1950s
And the clowns in Duffy's Circus
Have I laughed myself so sorry,
So sorry that I was ready to shout,
If anyone else had shouted:
'Stop Beckett! Stop McGovern!'

Even more explictly, Archbishop of Dublin to Film
Romeo and Juliet imagines the real, 1980s world of the
Irish Catholic hierarchy's interventions into politico-
sexual debates as a Beckettian drama:

The Archbishop of Dublin,
Inspired by the example of Saint Samuel Beckett
— We were told —

Will isolate Romeo and Juliet
In separate refrigerators:
Romeo in a refrigerator in Rome,
And Juliet in a refrigerator in Armagh;

These parallels with Beckett remind us that Paul Durcan's Ireland is a place at once real and absurd. For all the comic invention, all the dark exploration, of his work, Durcan is above all a great realist. He is a brilliant describer of a reality so dislocated, so imbued with political, religious and psychic myths, that it will not yield to prosaic language or to literal minds. The madness of his poetry is a realistic reflection of the mad Ireland that has stung him into it.

The realism of Durcan's work lies at one level in the simple fact that he noticed and noted more about Irish reality than most poets do. What he has noticed in particular is the gap between the way Ireland was supposed to be and the way it is. Because he is in thrall to none of the inherited orthodoxies of Irish writing — the preference for the country over the city, the belief in Ireland as a fixed frame for experience, the assumption that mundane reality is not fit material for poetry — Durcan shows a vivid awareness of social and economic realities. Two things above all lie behind his work — the rapid transformation of Ireland into an urban, industrial society in the 1960s and 1970s, and the extraordinary cultural porousness that resulted from this transformation. Paul Durcan is the poet of those fluid but inescapable facts.

The emergence of a new middle-class, whose identity is inseparable from material possessions, for instance, is captured in The National *Gallery Restaurant*:

I'd prefer to converse about her BMW — or my BMW —
Or the pros and cons of open plan in office-block
    architecture.

Or in *Tullynoe: Tete a Tete in the Parish Priest's Parlour,* where a dead man's life history is measured out in

automobiles:
... he was a grand man."
"He was: he had the most expensive Toyota you can
buy."
"He had: well it was only beautiful."
"It was: he used to have an Audi."
"He had: as a matter of fact he used to have two Audis."

Funny as such satires are, they allude to a world that is more real than invented. It is the world of a burgeoning middle-class Ireland whose culture is displaced and whose history can only be measured by the succession of cars. And just as time has lost its bearings, place has lost its reality:

We live in a Georgian, Tudor, Classical Greek,
Moorish, Spanish Hacienda, Regency Period
Ranch-House, Three-Storey Bungalow
On the edge of the edge of town:
'Poor Joe's Row' —
The townspeople call it —
But our real address is 'Ronald Reagan Hill',
— That vulturous-looking man in the States.

The movement of these lines, through a random succession of periods and places, through a landscape where even the names of places are unstable, where a woman starts to describe her home in Tipperary and ends up in the United States, could be called post-modern. But if Durcan is a post-modern writer, he is so for reasons far more profound than style. He writes out of a society that has become post-modern without ever really becoming modern, a place in which the global village is still a one-horse town. Durcan's Ireland is saturated with media imagery and has taken its place in cyberspace. But it is also stuck with peasant politics, an obscurantist church and with a mediaeval sectarian conflict on its doorstep.

Most powerfully, of course, this other, pre-modern Ireland is embodied for Durcan in the figure of his father. Because his father, as a judge,

> *The President of the Circuit Court*
> *Of the Republic of Ireland,*
> *Appointed by the party of Fine Gael*
> *served the State*
> *Unconditionally*
> *For twenty-eight years'*

there is no real dividing line between the public and private, the emotional and the political in his work. The State has for him a local habitation and a name, an intimate psychic presence that makes it far more than a collective abstraction. Public events in Ireland and elsewhere are refracted in many poems through the image of his father, the public man. In the process, Irish history becomes for Durcan both a dream and a nightmare.

As it is for Joyce's Stephen Daedalus, Irish history is for Durcan a nightmare from which he is trying to awake. But it is also a daydream, a wide-awake effort at re-imagining the past. Like Stephen, Durcan is also a wanderer in search of alternative fathers. Because his own father is both a personal and a political progenitor, he looks for other fathers that embody historic political alternatives to the Ireland we actually got. Ireland's political father-figure, Eamon de Valera, is pictured "blindly stalking us down" (*Making Love Outside Aras an Uachtarain*). Dismissed, he is replaced by a series of political figures with more capacity for contradiction, less for purity. Three deaths in March 1978 provide a coincidental but nonetheless sacred trinity of historic alternatives in Durcan's laments. Emmett Dalton, through whom the unlikely figures of Tom Kettle dying in the British Army in France and Michael Collins dying at Beal na mBlath, are united, is one such figure. Micheal MacLiammoir, who

> *dreamed a dream of Jean Cocteau*
> *Leaning against a wall in Kilnamoe*

is another. And the third is Cearbhall O Dalaigh,

> *A Gaelic Chinaman whose birthplace*
> *At 85 Main Street, Bray,*
> *Is today a Chinese Restaurant*
> *('The Jasmine' owned by Chi Leung Nam);*

Through such figures an alternative Irish history is imagined. But so, too, in Durcan's poems, is an alternative Irish geography, one in which France and Cork, France and Mayo, China and Bray, are neighbouring townlands. These unlikely conjunctions are the alternatives to Ronald Reagan Hill, in which the porous placelessness of modern Ireland is re-imagined not as a cultural nightmare but as a cause for celebration. And this is the point about Durcan's attitude to Ireland. He does not fly from the narrowness of Irish history or the absurdity of Irish geography. He imagines alternatives to them. And these alternatives are themselves rooted in Irish reality. They are made, not by pure invention, but by loosening the tongue of a hidden Ireland, allowing it to speak out its own unspoken complexities and richly contradictory possibilities.

This is at once an act of faith and of perception. Writing about Patrick Kavanagh, Paul Durcan remarked that "much of his work... demands of the reader spiritual courage as well as highly sensitive powers of perception..." That the same words could be used about Durcan himself is a reminder of the nature of his achievement. In his work, the power of seeing and the gift of believing go hand-in-hand. Wallace Stevens's definition of poetry as "an interdependence of the imagination and reality as equals" comes to mind. In Durcan's work, reality is always shaped and often transformed by the imagination. But it holds its place on equal terms. All writers try not to betray their own imaginative impulses. What distinguishes Paul Durcan is

187

that, at the same time, he tries equally not to betray reality.

He has never, for instance, followed the standard poetic belief that poetry is a kind of knowledge that is of a different order to journalistic reporting of reality. Durcan, in fact, goes very far indeed in aligning poetry with good reportage. In his early Tribute to a Reporter in Belfast, 1974, he not only pays homage to the work of RTE's Liam Hourican in his reports on the violence in Northern Ireland, but asks whether his 'uniquely utilitarian technique of truth-telling' might not be 'a poetry more/ than poetry is'. The question arises from a belief that language in Ireland has been abused 'and by poets as much as by gunmen or churchmen.' From this belief stems the essential commitment of all of Durcan's work — a commitment to a kind of poetry that does not abuse reality by abusing language. His quest can be said to be a search for a poetry that combines the integrity and the truth to life of the best journalism with the imaginative boldness of James Joyce or Patrick Kavanagh.

In this sense, Durcan is more concerned to describe his Ireland, to name it truthfully, than he is to poeticise it. His journalistic poems, in which he uses newspaper headlines and the form of the news report may be usually — though not always — satiric in intent. But it is always the kind of satire that conceives of itself in Swiftian terms as a magnification of reality so that we may see it the better.

The reality of Ireland is abundantly present in the poems. The most obvious thing about Durcan's work, indeed, is that in its range of both geographical and historical reference, it is unique. No living Irish poet and few dead ones can match the sheer range of Irish places reflected in the work. Three places are especially important — Dublin, Cork and Mayo — but an astonishing range of others makes its presence felt. Durcan is a national poet in the simple sense that his work touches on every part of Ireland — Lisdoonvarna, Cahir, Knock,

Armagh, Corofin, Belfast, Dun Chaoin, Racoo, Ballyferriter — in the process eluding the distinctions between North and South, between country and city.

In his continual naming of Irish places, Durcan is not a mere enumerator of points on a road map. Deeply embedded in his poetry is the idea that to name is to bless. In *Amnesty*, he recalls his father

> *For whom the names of places and people*
> *Are the signs by which he teaches me*
> *That they are holy and precious;*
> *That the plankton of all human life is mercy.*

Conversely, 'a place that does not have a name' — the prison — is 'not a holy and precious place'. The naming of so many places in Durcan's poems is thus an act of blessing and of mercy imbued with an intent far beyond that of creating a recognisable backdrop. His insistent naming of places that would otherwise have remained unnamed in poetry and therefore have been denied a recognition of their preciousness is one of the most important aspects of Durcan's care for Irish reality. He is the poet who, more than any other, has invented work capacious enough to articulate within its syntax the flotsam and jetsam of an Irish reality that had no place within the rural and romantic traditions of the Irish Revival.

Who else has named in poetry "the Asahi synthetic-fibre plant" (Backside to the Wind), Donnybrook Garage (*Margaret, Are You Grieving?*), Marks and Spencer's (*The Repentant Peter*), "the Pass Machine of the Bank of Ireland" in O'Connell Street (*Exterior With Plant*), "the Kentucky Grill" (*Chips*), the *National Gallery Restaurant*, the East Link Toll Bridge (*Dairine Vanston, 1903-1988* and *The Toll Bridge*), "The Bovril Sign, the Ballast Office Clock, the Broadstone" (*Hymn to My Father*)?

But Durcan is no mere poetic topographer. His Ireland is, in its own way, a holy Ireland. What makes it holy is the poet's ability to imbue its physical reality with the only blessings he knows — speech and sex. He makes Ireland both a suburb of Babel and an erogenous zone. The geography of Durcan's Ireland is the utopian geography of Joyce's Finnegans Wake in which Dublin is also the Dublin that is the county seat of Laurens County, Georgia, Baile Atha Cliath is also Balaclava, Dublin is also Lublin, the New Ireland is also the New Island (America), Crumlin is the Kremlin, West Munster is Westminster and the four provinces are 'used her, mused her, licksed her and cuddled.'

Landscape, in Durcan's work, is aroused to life both by being released from the confines of physical fixity and by being eroticised. The former is a political impulse, the latter a personal one, but as usual in his work they melt into each other. In this, he reflects realistically but imaginately, not only the facts of his own life but also the nature of contemporary Ireland as a cultural space forever hovering between America and Europe.

In *Before the Celtic Yoke*, Durcan imagines a literal geography, a writing of lands, in which physical reality becomes itself articulate, with 'verbs dripping fresh from geologic epochs'. In *The Mayo Accent*, speech and land become one as

Words are bog oak sunk in understatement;
Phrases are bog water in which syllables float...

The land is freed from the tyranny of its physical fixity and becomes ambiguous, infinitely capable of re-invention, as promiscuous and as slippery as language itself. Every place becomes sayable, every corner of Irish reality can be named, and thus find room in the utopian Babel that is Durcan's poetic homeland.

And just as Irish land can become articulate in Durcan, so too does it become imbued with sex. The landscape is frequently eroticised — perhaps the most profound mark of the influence of Kavanagh on Durcan: "the urban necklaces far below on the breast of the coastline" (EI Flight 106: New York to Dublin); 'the sea's thighs pillowing in' (*Martha's Wall*), "the hips of the Shannon estuary/ The pores of the gooseflesh of Ireland." (*Going Home To Russia*). In *O Westport in the Light of Asia Minor*

The islands come up through the mists
— Seductive garments that a man would dream of —

Just as the landscape can be humanised, so people can be assimilated to the landscape, as Nessa is in the vision of her as 'a whirlpool'. In *Hymn to Nessa*

Behind me on the sea shore Nessa lay
She is the red sun at nightfall

This may be a familiar poetic device, but it makes room for the central achievement of Durcan's realism, his invocation of an Ireland that is not a stable island, but a floating one. In his roles as priest and lover, blessing places and lusting after them, Durcan frees the land from its appearance of mute fixity. He comes as close as anyone has to describing the real cultural Ireland, a place that is not a point on the map, but rather closer to that humanised map that the cartographer Tim Robinson has described as a picture of the "nodes at which the layers of experience touch and may be fused together."

Place in Durcan is unstable, permeable, unbounded. Durcan's Ireland exists, not just in recognisable place-names, but in such surreal but meaningful places as "the east European parts of Dublin city", "the road from Mayo into Egypt", "Westport in the Light of Asia Minor", "Africa on the West Coast of Kerry", "the Kalahari, Pimlico, and the West of Ireland", "The Dublin-Paris-Berlin-Moscow Line", "a French Ireland".

These are the places of a poet who asks of "the history of transport — is there any other history?" (*Red Arrow*). For Durcan is, supremely, the poet, not just of emigration, but of a place constituted by its history of emigration. The American tourists in *Loosestrife in Ballyferriter* to whom

'Ireland is an odyssey odder than Iowa' are not too far in their sense of estrangement from a poet whose Ireland is, above all else, an odyssey, a journey, a history of transport. For not only is the Durcan of the poems continually in motion around Ireland and beyond it to Russia, America, France, Italy, Catalonia, and England, but the places themselves are continually shifting and melting into each other.

There are parallel universes on either edge of Europe, the Atlantic and the Caucasus. Poems placed in Ireland repeat themselves on the far side of Europe, as when *The Girl With the Keys to Pearse's Cottage* becomes *The Woman with the Keys to Stalin's House*, and *Going Home to Mayo* becomes *Going Home to Russia*. 'Home' is neither Mayo nor Moscow but both and therefore neither:

> *From the shores of the Aran Islands*
> *To the foothills the far side of the Caucasus*
> *These are the terraced streets*
> *That smell of home to us.*

Because of his profound sense of the instability of place, Durcan writes always as an exile, even when he is at home. He is 'the native who is an exile in his native land.' 'May I, a Dubliner, live always in exile', he prays in *The Dublin-Paris-Berlin-Moscow Line*. This sense of internal exile, of being both the one who stayed and the one who went, gives Durcan a special access to emigrant Ireland, to a place that is defined by its leavetakings. He writes directly of emigration in poems like The Girl With the Keys to Pearse's Cottage, and *Backside to the Wind*, where there are relatively conventional if also unusually moving images of young people forced to leave the West of Ireland. But he also, less conventionally, writes about Irish emigrants as part of a 'caravan of immigrants' (*The Deep Supermarket, Next Door to Ajay's*), taking their place in a migratory humanity marked *'by the relation of man and woman on this earth / Be / He or she / from Mayo or Sind...'*.

Emigration, in his work, is both a political fact and a spiritual state.

Because of emigration, Durcan's Ireland not merely has no fixed sense of place, but its history, both personal and national, is continually queasy with motion sickness. The man conceived in the toilets of the Cork-Dublin train (*The Boy Who Was Conceived in the Leithreas*), the couple making love in a Peugeot in a car wash (*High-Speed Car Wash*), the man who died falling out of train (*Tullynoe: Tete a Tete in the Parish Priest's Parlour*) are emblematic figures in Durcan's Ireland, images of 'having become the migrants that we are' (*The Dublin-Paris-Berlin-Moscow Line*). In his poems, Irish life from conception to death is lived in transit. Almost every poem takes place on the hoof — walking, driving, in a train, in a foreign city. And this is what makes him the national bard of the Republic of Elsewhere of which most Irish people are citizens.

One of the few Durcan poems that takes place entirely within a house, *Man Walking the Stairs*, happens on the stairs, the part of a house given over entirely to motion.

> *The whole point of my home*
> *Is the stairs. Can you conceive*
> *Of a life without stairs?*

The importance of Paul Durcan is that he can't. He lives, as a poet, neither downstairs in the foul rag and bone shop of the heart, nor upstairs in the realms of public history and culture, but on the stairs between them. He lives neither in the serene world of literary tradition nor in the demotic hurly-burly of sex and drugs and rock 'n' roll, but on the stairs between them. He lives neither in an immemorial Ireland of the past nor in an amnesiac Ireland of the present, but on the stairs between them. Stairs are awkward, bumpy, irregular and angular places to live on, hard to get up and easy to fall down. Paul Durcan's

willingness to endure poetic life in such places makes him
the man with the keys to the Irish tower of Babel.

The Way We Are

Scenes From The Birth Of A New Morality

A Catholic priest, Father Brendan Smyth, has been convicted in Belfast of sexually abusing children. Chris Moore's television documentary has revealed that Smyth's career of crime had lasted since the 1950s, and that he had been shielded by the Church authorities. The head of the Irish Catholic Church, Cardinal Cahal Daly, had known of some of Smyth's offences before his arrest, but failed to call in the police. (This piece was written in November 1994.)

Anyone with half a heart listening to Cardinal Cahal Daly on RTE's This Week radio programme last Sunday would have felt real sympathy for the man, when he confessed that the child abuse scandal currently unfolding had brought him beyond the brink of tears. It is not easy for men to cry, and it is even harder for public men of the Cardinal's generation to talk openly about the shedding of tears.

For a man who carries such a weight of public authority, and who has learned over many years in the cockpit of violent confrontation to be guarded in expressing his feelings, the sudden revelation of those emotions was dramatic. Dramatic but appropriate — for it acknowledged, in a way that more abstract language could not have done, the sheer scale of the crisis that faces both the Catholic Church and Dr Daly himself.

The trauma of the case of Father Brendan Smyth and his 40-year career of paedophilia is immeasurably deepened by the fact that the case itself, in a sense, reveals nothing. A revelation is stunning and unexpected. It alters the known shape of reality.

But the Smyth case is more a confirmation than a revelation. Rather than changing what we know about reality, it confirms it. It puts a face to the dark, faceless knowledge that has clung to Irish childhood for generations. It names a nameless truth.

At the level of raw experience, hundreds of thousands of people in Ireland have known for most of their lives that there is a problem of paedophilia within the Church. Ask anyone who attended a boy's school in Ireland and they will tell you that while most of the teachers were decent and professional there was always one brother or priest who was regarded as a bit of a menace.

The risk of being molested was taken for granted. Because of corporal punishment, the normal rules of acceptable behaviour on the part of adults in authority were understood to be suspended once you went through the school gates. Being beaten and being molested were not, from the child's point of view, fundamentally different risks. If the adult world permitted one, there was no reason to believe that it would object to the other.

But to this general knowledge has been added in recent years a growing body of first-hand testimony of much more serious abuse in residential institutions run by the Church. There was Mannix Flynn's account in *Nothing to Say* of his time in Letterfrack industrial school. There was Paddy Doyle's account in *The God Squad* of his period in an industrial school. Doyle recalled the mixture of brutality and cajoling, distorted sexuality so typical of child abuse, in his case visited on him by a nun who ran the institution.

Perhaps most disturbing of all is Patrick Touher's memoir of his life in Artane industrial school, Fear of the

Collar. Touher's account is particularly disturbing because it is written by someone who, unlike Doyle or Flynn, clearly retained a great deal of affection for the Christian Brothers, for the institution and for the Church.

One day, he and two classmates wandered out of bounds to collect conkers. They were caught by one of the brothers. The brother beat the other two boys first and then told Touher to come to his room that night. While he was waiting, the other two boys told him that the brother had molested them while beating them. That evening Touher, then aged nine, went to the brother's room. He was stripped, beaten, molested, whipped, and then molested again, the brother promising 'I'll protect you, I promise, I will never beat you again. I will be like a father to you."

These three books were published in 1983, 1988 and 1991. They were about the past, and nobody, neither Cardinal Daly nor anyone else, can pundo the past. But what those in authority can and should do is to try to make sure that the past remains the past, that the suffering inflicted on innocent children in the 1950s and 1960s would alert the Church to the dangers of the 1980s and 1990s. For even if it were possible the Church authorities were not aware of the presence of paedophiles and abusers within their ranks before, they could not, after the publication of these grim testimonies, claim ignorance now.

Instead, the knowledge that child abuse within the Church was a long-term and widespread fact of life, known but not acknowledged, seems to have had the opposite effect. If the case of Father Brendan Smyth had been isolated, there is little doubt that the Church would have dealt with it effectively and quickly.

But because it was a tangible symptom of a much larger malaise, there seems to have been a sense that it was best not to make an issue of it, lest the issue become an unbearably big one.

In this context, it is easy to understand and to feel personal sympathy for the grief of Cardinal Daly. But it is also important to remember that the Cardinal is not, in this story, just a private figure or even a spiritual leader. He is also the leader of an organisation which holds, and insists on its right to hold, huge temporal power on this island. In particular he is the leader of an organisation which claims wide-ranging rights over the education and welfare of children.

As a private man he is entitled to sympathy. As a spiritual leader he is entitled to respect. But as the wielder of temporal power, he is subject to the same kind of social accountability as anyone else in a similiar position. And so far, he has given a poor account of his stewardship in this affair. It is not good enough that he should give a bureaucratic explanation about the chain of command, and his own inability to intervene in the affairs of the Norbertine Order. The trust that Father Smyth played on and betrayed was trust in the Church, not in the Norbertines. Passing the buck down the line like any cornered politician will not restore that trust.

Cardinal Daly's own tears should tell him that the scale and depth of this problem cannot be brushed aside with the language of the bureaucrat or the politician. This crisis is about fundamental things — power, exploitation, authority. It shows what happens in any institution — political, religious or social — where people are taught to obey without question, to accept orders, to do what they are told out of fear and shame and to keep their mouths shut. If the Church is to show that it is no longer such an institution, it must start by speaking more openly and more courageously about the lessons it has learned from these terrible events.

✦ ✦ ✦ ✦ ✦

November 1994. The consequences of the Brendan Smyth affair spread from Church to State. The Attorney General Harry Whelehan fails to explain delays in processing a request for Smyth's extradition to the satisfaction of the Labour party, which pulls out of Government. The Fianna Fail leader Albert Reynolds loses office just at the moment of his greatest triumph, his role in bringing about the short-lived IRA ceasefire.

Early last Thursday, as Ireland was waking to the morning after its wildest political night for decades, I met at Heathrow Airport one of the grand old men of Fianna Fail. Throughout the upheavals within the party in the 1980s, he was one of those who would appear on television to make announcements, to steady nerves, to reassure the public. Now, he was walking along an airport corridor pushing a trolley and shaking his head with an air of unfathomable perplexity.

We spoke for a few minutes, but he couldn't find much to say. He had left Ireland a fortnight ago, leaving behind a government with the largest majority in the history of the State and a Taoiseach on the brink of delivering a historic end to the political violence that has seemed endemic to Irish life for a century. Now he was going back to a collapsed government, a disgraced Taoiseach, and a senior judge under pressure to resign, all against the background of a child abuse scandal involving a Catholic priest. The only thing he could be sure of, he said, was that he was glad he no longer had the job of explaining things.

It was easy to agree. For bizarre as the events themselves had been, what was still more amazing was the fact that, for much of Wednesday, the most fantastic rumours had been believed in Dublin. When the Dail met to debate a motion of confidence in Albert Reynolds the Democratic Left TD Pat Rabbitte rose to allege that there was a letter in the Attorney General's office whose contents would rock the State to its foundations. Between then and the emergence of the rather more prosaic fact that the

Attorney General's office had, contrary to the impression given to the Dail by Albert Reynolds on Tuesday, dealt previously with a similar case to the Brendan Smyth one, this claim spawned an extraordinary brood of rumours.

These rumours implicated the very highest levels of both Church and State in scandal, forcing the head of the Irish Church, Cardinal Cahal Daly, to go on television to denounce suggestions that he had tried to interfere with the prosecution of the paedophile priest Father Brendan Smyth as 'absurd'. Wild as many of the rumours were, though, they revealed a deeper truth — that the Irish public was now so alienated from those in authority that it was prepared to believe almost anything. How had such complete mistrust taken hold in what used to be one of the most conservative and deferential societies in Europe?

This was, after all, once the society in which the dominant politician Eamon de Valera, the founder of Fianna Fail, could say with evident sincerity that whenever he wanted to know what the Irish people were thinking he had only to look into his own heart. It was the society in which, while the Second Vatican Council was shaking Catholic belief, the Archbishop of Dublin could return home from Rome to tell his flock that there was nothing in the Council which should disturb the tranquillity of the faithful in Ireland. It was the society in which, as recently as 1986, the combined authority of the Church and Fianna Fail could still defeat proposals to permit divorce. Last Wednesday, it was a society in which people seemed prepared to assume the worst about both of those institutions.

The Irish novelist Flann O'Brien began his surreal novel *At Swim-Two-Birds* with the announcement that there was no reason why a story should have only one beginning, and that his would have three. The story of a surreal week in Irish politics has at least as many beginnings.

One of them is the revelation in 1992 that the Catholic Bishop of Galway, Eamon Casey had fathered a son and had used church funds to pay for his upkeep. The erosion of the authority of the Church since that revelation is one of the ingredients of this week's events. Out of it emerges the most shadowy but nonetheless the most potent figure in the drama, Fr Brendan Smyth, the Catholic priest serving a jail sentence in Northern Ireland for sexual offences against children.

A second beginning is in April, 1987, when Albert Reynolds as Minister for Industry and Commerce in a minority Fianna Fail government led by Charles Haughey began a series of dealings with one of the country's most powerful private citizens, the beef baron Larry Goodman. Between then and late 1989, Mr Goodman received from that government an extraordinary series of benefits, most notably $100 million of export credit insurance for his exports to Iraq. The gradual revelation of these dealings in a three-year public inquiry, which finally reported last August, created the climate of suspicion between Albert Reynolds and his deputy in the coalition government, Dick Spring, in which this week's events unfolded.

The third beginning, and the one in which the issues of Church and State in the other two are brought together is the infamous X case of 1992. In that case Albert Reynolds's newly- appointed Attorney General, Harry Whelehan took out a High Court injunction to prevent a 14 year-old girl, pregnant as a result of rape, from leaving Ireland to have an abortion in England. The X case suddenly brought to attention the hitherto unnoticed fact that the low-profile office of Attorney General was one in which the separate areas of law, politics, morality, and religion could collide with the most dramatic consequences. The X case turned Harry Whelehan overnight from an obscure lawyer into a figure around whom many of the most visceral emotions in Irish life — the deep divisions between conservatives and liberals — converged. It ensured that Albert Reynolds's determination to appoint him to the second most senior judicial post in the country, the presidency of the High Court, would not, as such appointments usually are, be a matter for public indifference.

If the story has three beginnings, though, it has one theme — the collapse of authority. Behind the breathtakingly rapid series of events is a slower shift in the nature of Irish society. As Ireland has moved in recent decades from a largely rural and traditional society to a largely modern and urban one, the relationship of its people to power has changed. Quite simply, a young, highly educated and largely urban population is not prepared to accept that the exercise of power in Ireland is none of its business.

That change, though, was seldom obvious. The big monoliths of the culture stayed in place. Fianna Fail, the party which had been in power for most of the history of the State, stayed in power. The Church which had wielded even greater authority, both spiritual and temporal, for even longer, continued, outwardly at least, to enjoy the faith and trust of a large majority of the population. These apparent continuities, though, hid an essential fact — that the public now regarded its loyalties as conditional on the behaviour of those in power. The problem was that those in power did not grasp this change.

The Church, for its part, failed to understand that the Casey affair was more than a shocking aberration. If anything, Bishop Casey's fall from grace looked by the beginning of this week in November 1994 like a golden memory from an innocent past. On Monday, the three big stories on Irish radio and television news were the political repercussions of the Father Brendan Smyth case; the death of a Dublin priest in a gay sauna (fortunately, two other priests were on hand to give him the last rites), and the conviction of a Galway priest for a sexual assault on a young man. What was significant was not that these events had occurred, but that they had come into the public domain. The hypocrisies and failings which had always been present within the Church were now coming into the open.

The failure of the Church to understand what was happening was revealed with stark clarity in the Brendan Smyth affair. What emerged after Smyth's conviction in Belfast this summer was that he had been abusing children in Britain, Ireland and America since the 1950s. Each time he was sent to a parish, whispers of scandal would begin to emerge. Each time, he would be sent back to Ireland, and then posted off to another parish. Over four decades, the Church authorities treated his behaviour as an internal affair to be dealt with by admonition or attempts at medical treatment, not as a criminal matter in which the law of the State should have any remit.

The unspoken, perhaps unconscious, belief that the power of the Church was somehow beyond and above the power of the State comes through most strongly in a letter from Cardinal Daly to the family of one of Smyth's victims in Belfast:

'There have been complaints about this priest before, and once I had to speak to the superior about him. It would seem that there has been no improvement. I shall speak with the superior again.' The idea that the appropriate people to speak to might be the police rather than the superior of Father Smyth's Norbertine Order does not seem to have occurred to the Cardinal. Even in the 1990s, the Church had not grasped the fact that most Irish people now find such notions of unaccountable authority intolerable. But then neither had the State, or, more precisely, the State's vicar on earth, Fianna Fail. While Father Brendan Smyth's long career of abusing power and trust was beginning to break the surface of discreet silence, Fianna Fail's use of power was also coming under scrutiny. The tribunal of inquiry into the beef processing industry was producing tangible, if complicated, evidence of a murky relationship between politics, business and the administration of the State. If the details of Albert

Reynolds's central role in the affair were difficult for the public to grasp, the talk of private meetings and secret policies, of large benefits for a powerful businessman in a period of severe cutbacks in public spending, created an atmosphere of mistrust. For the first time, the public was given a glimpse of how decisions are actually made in government departments, and what they saw did nothing to enhance the authority of senior politicians.

Ironically, the peace process itself was part of a wider momentum in the island as a whole, one that is at odds with Albert Reynolds's attempts to use it to avoid accountability. That momentum is towards democracy, and away from all forms of private power, whether it be the brute force of private armies, the subtle hints of senior churchmen, or the discreet intimacies of the Cabinet room. The irony is that Gerry Adams grasped the shift in the public attitude to authority more clearly than either Cardinal Daly or Albert Reynolds did.

Far from damaging the peace process, the events of this week have enhanced it. A new settlement in Ireland will only be possible if ideas like democracy, accountability, consent and trust are given real meaning. This week, both Church and State have been given painful lessons in what those meanings should be.

◆ ◆ ◆ ◆ ◆

December 1995. In the fallout from the crisis, Fianna Fail looks like falling apart.

Seldom in peacetime can a parliament have heard a description of a government in action quite like that of the Attorney General, Eoghan Fitzsimons, read out in the Dail last Tuesday:

"It appeared to me that the Fianna Fail ministers were behaving in a very disorganised manner. No-one appeared to be in charge. At the meetings I attended, Ministers came in and out at will, with some being absent for periods."

Even more remarkable was the fact that this vision of chaos was conjured up by a long-time party supporter and activist. Eoghan Fitzsimons was once a member of Fianna Fail's Committee of Fifteen — the trustee, not just of a political party, but of The Spirit of the Nation.

More remarkable still was the fact that this was not a condemnation but a plea in mitigation, the best that could be said about the behaviour of the leadership of Fianna Fail in the week beginning November 14th last. Far from seeking to deny it, some of those same ministers have embraced this description of their own state of mind with considerable enthusiasm, anxiously claiming confusion, tiredness, and even stupidity as desirable epithets.

Nor was the chaos confined to that fateful week. This week too it has been played out live on screen for the nation's delectation. The Spirit of the Nation has descended into a hell of fear and loathing. In the last few days, we have seen a Fianna Fail Taoiseach 'categorically' and bitterly reject any suggestion that the former Fianna Fail Attorney General Harry Whelehan, the man he appointed to the second most senior judicial office in the State, ever set foot in his apartment, as if the very notion were repellent.

We have heard the Fianna Fail Minister for Justice openly contradict the present Fianna Fail Attorney General. We have been treated to the extraordinary spectacle of the Government Information Service ringing in to RTE's *Prime Time* programme on Tuesday night to claim that the blame for putting through the estimates for government expenditure last week while Fianna Fail and Labour were still in negotiation about the formation of a new government lay with Bertie Ahern and not with Albert Reynolds. We have had Ray Burke thundering his denunciations of Albert Reynolds to Charlie Bird.

Fianna Fail is then, by its own account and on the clear evidence of the behaviour of its own senior figures in a state of utter disarray. The chaos within the party and the

damage done to the reputations of virtually its entire
upper echelon are so profound as to prompt a question that
would have seemed ludicrous even four years ago. Is
Fianna Fail, one of the world's most successful democratic
parties, about to go the way of some of the other great
ruling political monoliths — the Italian Christian
Democrats, Japan's Liberal Democratic Party, the
Communist Party of the Soviet Union, the Congress Party
in India — and enter a period of terminal decline?

For Fianna Fail, the events of the last few weeks,
horrendous as they have been, would be much less serious
if they were much more like the last time a Fianna Fail
Attorney General dominated the news, when the murderer
Malcolm McArthur was found in Patrick Connolly's flat in
1982. That occurrence was genuinely grotesque,
unbelievable, bizarre and unprecedented, a wild accident
of fate. Those at the top of the party now would like to
believe that recent events are of the same order. The very
attraction of the idea of confusion, even of stupidity, to
those involved suggests that there is for them some bleak
form of comfort in the idea that it all happened because of
grotesque but unpredictable human failings.

This is, of course, partly because it is better to be judged
stupid than corrupt. But it is also a natural reaction to
disaster. When a plane crashes into the side of a mountain,
it is somehow more comforting to be told that the accident
resulted from pilot error than from structural flaws in the
aircraft's guidance system. All week, Fianna Fail's pilot,
co-pilot, chief stewardess and maintenance crews have
been blaming each other for the disaster. Painful as this
is, it is much more pleasant than facing the fact that the
machine was not just badly handled but may also have
built-in flaws which will prevent it from getting off the
ground again.

The hard truth is that what is most remarkable about
recent events is not that they occurred, but that they were
so long delayed. Fianna Fail has been in serious disarray

since the trauma of Charles Haughey's coup against Jack Lynch in 1979.

That putsch, and the public bickering within the party ever since, has gradually eroded the very core of Fianna Fail's appeal — the mystical but powerfully effective charisma of the National Movement.

In his now famous 1981 *ard-fheis* address, Mr. Haughey told the faithful in strikingly religious terms, that they got the support of the people because Fianna Fail 'represents not this pressure group or that sectional interest, this class or that creed, but because in the broad sweep of its membership and their faith and devotion to their own country, there resides what one can well call 'the spirit of the nation'.

The Spirit of the Nation does not need to argue or explain, or even to answer questions in the Dail with any frankness.

The party does not justify itself to the people, is not accountable, because it is the people, or at least the people who matter, the real Irish people. 'This ard-fheis,' Mr. Haughey told his congregation in 1984, ' speaks with the authentic voice of Irish Ireland". And for a long time, this authentic voice of Irish Ireland could be merged with P.J. Mara's *Uno Duce, Una Voce*. As Ray Burke declared in 1982 during one of the heaves against Haughey: 'Loyalty to Fianna Fail is loyalty to the nation itself and its social and economic progress." And since loyalty to the party was loyalty to its leader, then expecting the party leadership to account for its use of power was virtually an act of treason against the nation.

This powerful ideology has been undermined in recent years by three inter-related forces. One is the long-term and global trend away from monolithic identifications in the kind of complex western society that Ireland has become. A second is the diminishing resonance of the broader cultural symbols that Fianna Fail drew on — nationalism, Catholicism and the Irish language. The third, and most fatal, is the obvious and naked division within the party itself since 1979. Whatever chance a united, coherent Fianna Fail might have had of surviving the long-term changes in Irish society intact, a party riven by uncivil wars had none. When the authentic voice of Irish Ireland is in reality a bickering Tower of Babel, it can no longer speak with authority.

Throughout the 1990s, the public has been treated to the most dramatic images of Fianna Fail at odds with itself. The unceremonial shafting of Brian Lenihan when he became an embarrassment during the 1990 presidential election campaign; the comedy of Gerry Collins's live television appeal to Albert Reynolds not to 'burst up the party'; the ruthless use of hints about Bertie Ahern's private life dropped by Michael Smith and Albert Reynolds himself in the 1992 leadership contest — such moments dispelled once and for all the image of a mystical union by which Fianna Fail had avoided the need to answer for its actions.

Even worse, with the passing of Charles Haughey, Fianna Fail no longer possessed a figure capable of sustaining interest in the division of the political world into the elect and the damned, the National Movement and the traitors, on which the party's aura had depended. The idea of Irish politics as a permanent fixture between Fianna Fail and a World XV was undermined by the coalition with the Progressive Democrats in 1989, and shattered by the coalition with Labour. Fianna Fail was just another political party, but one whose whole culture denied the need to account for its actions.

What is striking in retrospect about the advent of Albert Reynolds is that those around him were not blind to what was happening to the party. If Albert Reynolds himself lacked perspicuity, his ablest lieutenants Maire Geoghegan-Quinn and Padraig Flynn did not. There is no reason to doubt the sincerity of their public statements in early 1992 about the need to 'let in the light', about a new spirit of openness and about their desire for the party to take a hard look at itself.

Whatever their desires, however, they lacked the capacity to fulfil them. In broad terms, Fianna Fail did not have the intellectual resources to come up with a new ideological direction.

The consequences of these problems were made clear in the dreadful performance of the party in the 1992 election. But for the extraordinary intervention of Dick Spring to save Albert Reynolds by going into coalition with him, the party would have been able to face those consequences in opposition.

Instead, it was placed back in power with all of its fundamental problems frozen in place. Salvaged from the judgement of the electorate, Fianna Fail was lulled into complacency, forgetting the truths about the state of the party that even Albert Reynolds had acknowledged when he first became leader.

The National Movement has been irreparably destroyed, and the task of re-inventing Fianna Fail as an ordinary democratic political party is now much more difficult than it was even two years ago. For one thing, Bertie Ahern has to begin that task in an atmosphere of bitter recrimination and with his own reputation and those of almost all of his senior colleagues badly tarnished.

For another, the emergence of a strong centre ground consensus in Irish politics, with Fianna Fail, Labour and Fine Gael all occupying similar political territory makes it very difficult to construct a coherent opposition while still maintaining a catch-all appeal. Just as John Bruton found it very difficult in the last two years to find a clear line of attack on the Fianna Fail-Labour consensus, so too will Bertie Ahern, all the more so since any new coalition will almost certainly be implementing a programme which Fianna Fail was already committed to in its partnership with Labour. A new leader of Fianna Fail starting out with a good stock of political capital would find that task formidable. A new leader whose political capital has already been dramatically devalued may well find it impossible.

❖ ❖ ❖ ❖ ❖

June 1995. The secret life of Ireland's most famous Catholic priest, Father Michael Cleary, a passionate defender of conservative values until his death in December 1994, has been revealed. He had fathered two children with his 'housekeeper' (in fact his common-law wife) Phyllis Hamilton. Bishop Brendan Comiskey hints that it may be time for a debate on clerical celibacy.

"Gossip", wrote the late Andrew Kopkind, "serves as justice in a corrupt world." In a piece about Kitty Kelley's scurrilous biography of Nancy Reagan (included in a terrific recent collection of his writing, The Thirty Years' Wars), Kopkind noted that "In a more perfect place, Nancy Reagan would have been brought to trial for crimes against sincerity, candour and taste, and surely judgement would have been terrible and swift. The United States penal code, however, omits such offences, so there's only Kitty Kelley to even the scales."

In a more perfect place, too, Father Michael Cleary's lapses of taste, his coarsening effect on Irish public life, his substitution of crude propaganda for reasoned argument would have been more than enough to tarnish his reputation. Instead, we are left with gossip as a pale and inadequate substitute for justice. Yet again, we see the public realm — the arena of social responsibility and political participation — shrink into the private domain of sexuality and property.

Yet again, too, we have to put up with the fantasy that the saga of Michael Cleary has something to do with a confrontation between the media and the Church. The Church's response to anything in the media has now become so automatically one of blank denial that Bishop

Brendan Comiskey has to publicly deny the ridiculous claim of Cardinal Daly that the former's remarks on celibacy had been 'taken out of context' in media reports. By blaming the media, the very existence of a real problem and a real debate can be blithely denied.

Equally, Church sources now talk as if Michael Cleary himself had not been, first and foremost, a media personality. He had, lest it be forgotten, a column in the *Sunday Independent* for five years. He then had a column in *The Star*. And he had, for four years, an hour-long, five nights a week phone-in show on 98FM. He was a clergyman in the same sense that the Reverend Ian Paisley is — a man who brings the aura of religious authority into public life.

And in that public life as a journalist and broadcaster, he showed no reluctance to encourage the worst tendencies of tabloid journalism — the conflation of journalism and show business, the substitution of emphatic assertion for verifiable fact, the repetition of paranoid fantasies as public truths. Especially on the most difficult public issue of abortion, he engaged in staggeringly insensitive stunts.

During a televised debate on the 1983 abortion referendum, he made the wildest of connections between the wording of a constitutional amendment and the obliteration of people with disabilities by drawing attention to a young woman in a wheelchair. He later described his own methods of ensuring that the presenter John Bowman introduced this woman into the programme: "I actually went over to him during a commercial break and I said 'If you don't call her, I'm going to push her out in front of the cameras.'"

Ten years later, on his 98FM radio show, Michael Cleary used the opportunity of an interview with Mother Teresa to make vile allegations about the family at the centre of the *X* case, saying that the case was "a model... planned deliberately to test the amendment" and that he suspected a great deal of organisation behind it.

This was a grotesque falsehood, made all the worse by the fact that he associated the moral authority of Mother Teresa, who clearly knew nothing about the reality of the X case, with it. It was a vastly more abusive and nastier allegation than anything the *Sunday World* has written about Michael Cleary. It implied the most disgusting conduct on the part, not merely of lawyers, journalists and Supreme Court judges, but much more importantly of an innocent and abused child. By comparison, an allegation that a man fathered children in a consensual and loving relationship, even if it were untrue, pales into insignificance. When it came to giving scandal, Michael Cleary needed no lessons. And if, as Father Cleary's friends now suggest, it is wrong to make allegations against someone who cannot defend himself, how much worse was it to make allegations against a family which could only identify itself by exposing a hurt child to the public gaze?

The point is not that one bad turn deserves another, but that, in his career as a journalist and broadcaster, Michael Cleary is at least as responsible as anyone else for the coarsening of public discourse to the point where we now have a dead man's Valentine cards reproduced in full colour in a national newspaper. And he carried that crudity into his belief that the public good, the political arena, should be defined by people like himself.

When, in the abortion debate, even the Catholic hierarchy was recognising 'the right of each person to vote according to conscience', Michael Cleary was telling priests in his *Sunday Independent* column to "start this Sunday by telling your people about life and its origins... Tell them to vote 'yes' and make no apology for it." Later, after the divorce referendum, he boasted that "individual priests like myself" made all the running, while "the bishops were very soft". The sheer vulgarity of such an approach to political debate, flattening out even the subtleties and complexities of his own Church's position, did a great deal to coarsen public life in Ireland.

Gossip may be rough justice, but in the case of Michael Cleary it may be justice nonetheless, not as an eye for an eye but as a reminder of just why it is so wrong to treat public issues with crass moral absolutism. If it is true that Ireland's best-known priest had a lover and children, it just might convince some people that human realities can never be reduced to mere sloganising. In public, Michael Cleary said things like "The Church can alter certain regulations and laws that it makes itself, but it can't change the laws of God. We give the maker's instructions and we can't bend them — they're not ours to bend." In private, it seems, that unbending certainty was abandoned.

What can be abandoned in private should also be abandoned in public. It is not too late in Ireland to create a public realm in which debate is free of paranoia, scandal-mongering and the pulling of religious rank. The courage of Bishop Brendan Comiskey in trying to drag the Church into a new era of calm and open discussion of controversial issues is a good start. But it has been met with the usual conspiracy theories. Cardinal Daly has hinted at "a campaign" in "some sectors of the media", referring, I presume, to the Catholic magazine *Reality*, which in its May issue reported a survey of its readers, most of whom are committed Catholics aged over 50 and 63 per cent of whom believe that it is time to end mandatory celibacy for priests. If, in spite of the Cardinal's refusal to see what is front of his nose, Bishop Comiskey and his allies manage to establish a new kind of public discourse in the Church, they will help to create an atmosphere in which justice will not need gossip to do its dirty work for it.

✦ ✦ ✦ ✦ ✦

August 1995. An abandoned baby is buried on the west coast of Ireland.

On Wednesday morning, a child was buried in the churchyard in Waterville, County Kerry, under a gravestone marked "Finian", in honour of the local saint. He was a little boy, found dead on the strand by a local man and his son, out for an early morning walk. The funeral had been arranged by the Garda and the priest, the representatives, if you like, of State and Church, the big powers of Irish society disposing of an anonymous child of an anonymous and unknown mother and father.

Ten years ago, such a scene would have been a metaphor for all that was despicable about Irish society. Then, a burial like that of baby Finian could only have been seen through the blood-tinted spectacles of the Kerry Babies inquiry which had taken its final submissions a few weeks earlier. Finian would have reminded us all of the baby boy found in similar circumstances in April 1984, on White Strand, just a few miles from Waterville.

The discovery of that baby, of course, had led to a bitterly shameful episode in which an innocent woman was charged with murder, and four members of her family were charged with concealing a birth of an unnamed male child. This in turn led to a protracted public inquiry that descended, as the Garda put forward increasingly bizarre theories to justify their behaviour, into the grotesque, with the woman who had been the victim in the affair becoming the object of hysterical slander. The Kerry Babies episode became not just an exposure of religious hypocrisy and State incompetence, but itself a shameful symptom of a society's sickness.

Yet, if it is a metaphor at all, the burial of baby Finian on Wednesday is one with a very different meaning. The fact that there are still dead babies in the beaches and fields of Ireland — there have been similar incidents in Listowel and Drimoleague this year— reminds us, indeed, that for all the talk of a brave new Ireland, there is still a strong current of fear and shame beneath the apparently calm surface of our morality. But within that awful continuity, the change in attitudes could hardly be more profound.

It is now obvious, however tacitly, that Irish society no longer treats the death of an abandoned infant as a crime requiring prosecution and punishment. On Morning Ireland on Wednesday morning, a Garda made it clear that the force's only concern in trying to trace the mothers of such babies is to make sure that they are getting the necessary medical and psychological help and to 'close the book' on the investigation. In the case of the Listowel and Drimoleague babies, this has been done.

In the case of baby Finian, the burial was held off for weeks in the hope that the mother might come forward and that her own wishes for the funeral might be respected. The name on the gravestone and the place of burial have been widely broadcast, so that the mother, whether or not she ever chooses to come forward, may in the future be able to visit the grave. These are basic courtesies, but in a society where until quite recently unbaptised infants were buried in unmarked graves in unconsecrated ground between sunset and sunrise, they are eloquent evidence of something that it is often hard to notice: that Ireland is becoming a more civilised place.

The striking thing about these new attitudes on the part of State and Church is that, in spite of all the bitter divisions in Ireland on issues of personal morality, it would be hard to find anyone to stand up and say that the Garda are showing a disgracefully lax attitude to the law, or that women who actively or passively contribute to the deaths of their infants should in fact be prosecuted and punished. Instinctively, anyone who is not a complete crank knows that morality and respect for the law are enhanced rather than undermined by the merciful compassion that is now shown to women in these circumstances.

And yet, even though almost everyone agrees that this is the case, almost everyone is equally loathe to say on what grounds this should be so, or to spell out the general principles that make it right. What we have, after all, is a deliberate and apparently systematic policy of not applying the law. Under the Infanticide Act of 1949, a woman suspected by the police of having killed her baby should be charged with murder. Equally, a parent who neglects or abandons a child commits a serious criminal offence. So what does it tell us when we think it right that these serious laws should be effectively and publicly placed on one side?

It tells us, I think, two very important things, each of which has an important bearing on the development of a society that is both civilised and pluralist. The first is that people can be better than the law, that we need to stop thinking of the law of the land as the be all and end all of our morality. The second is that, when it comes to the big issues of life and death, we are much more decent, and much more sophisticated, than we give ourselves credit for.

Social conservatives take an essentially pessimistic view of the relationship between the way people behave and the way the law says they should behave. They believe that the law should set a very high but immutable standard for behaviour. They know, of course that many people will fall short of this standard but they think that, if the standard were lowered or removed, we would go the dogs altogether. They therefore argue that, however many 'hard cases' there may be, it is better to keep the law in place and to see it through.

Yet the profound change in the way we treat abandoned babies and their mothers utterly contradicts this notion. The effective suspension of the law, far from making for more bad behaviour, has made us, as a society, behave infinitely better than we did even a decade ago. Though it should not have taken the burning at the stake of Joanne Hayes to make it happen, the fact is that we do now behave with more compassion, more sensitivity, more tenderness towards hurt women. We behave, in other words, more morally. We have discovered in at least one area of Irish life — a very difficult and traumatic one at that — that less law can mean more morality.

Or rather, to be more accurate, this is not so much a discovery as an admission. One of the strange things about Ireland is that, perhaps uniquely among societies, we have insisted on proclaiming a public morality that is in many ways worse than our private values. Our peculiar form of hypocrisy has been not a whitened but a blackened sepulchre, proclaiming to the world a rigid, intolerant, heartless face that belies the actual decency and humanity of the way ordinary Irish people tend to look upon people in trouble. If we can continue to construct laws that reflect our better selves, the new gravestone in Waterville churchyard may serve, not just as a sad memorial to an Ireland we are still trying to escape from, but also as a signpost to a society that could offer a decent home to the likes of little Finian.

✦ ✦ ✦ ✦ ✦

November 1995 — the morning after the referendum to remove the prohibition on divorce, the last specifically Catholic clause, from the Irish Constitution.

Dr T.K. Whitaker, one of the prime movers in the creation of modern Ireland, once visited the shrines of Irish saints on the European continent, among them Saint Gall at St Gallen and Saint Virgilius at Salzburg. He was delighted to find that they shared their altars with local saints — Gall with a Saint Otmar and Virgilius with a Saint Ruprecht. "I suppose", he joked in a lecture in 1977, "Irish initiative and devotion needed eventually to be underpinned by German organisation and method!"

It was, if you were opening Ireland to all the uncertainties and discontinuities of the modern world, as Dr Whitaker and Sean Lemass did in the 1960s, a comforting image. On the altar of Catholicism, Irish devotion could sit side by side in mutual comfort with the method and organisation of industrial modernity. The most sweeping changes in politics, the economy and society, could be undertaken in the belief that a core of tradition, contained above all within the Catholic faith, would remain unaltered. Change would underpin Irish devotion, not undermine it. Therefore change was not to be feared but to be embraced.

In this sense, religious devotion in Ireland was not the enemy of social change but one of the main things that facilitated it. It provided a layer of continuity that helps to explain why Ireland has coped so well with all the confusion and uncertainty of moving from a very predictable society to a very open and unpredictable one. And perhaps one of the lessons of the divorce debate is that the opposite is also true: that in a time of crisis for the Catholic church, it is harder, not easier, for Catholics to cope with the idea of change.

Until recently, the relative stability of Irish Catholicism was truly remarkable. While almost everything was changing, the practice of the Catholic faith remained largely intact. Ireland joined the EU and developed a society closely comparable to other European democracies in lifestyles, sexual behaviour, and social problems. But over eighty per cent of Catholics in the Republic still attend Mass at least once a week, compared to less than half in Spain and Italy, and less than one in eight in France.

Precisely because Ireland has been changing so rapidly, the Church represented for many people the last bastion of stability and security. Those who favoured social change always saw the church, for obvious reasons, as a barrier to progress. Yet the divorce debate has shown that even with the institutional church at its weakest for 150 years, there is still massive resistance to change. Whatever the outcome of the vote, this should force everyone to re-think the relationship between religion and politics in Ireland.

The institutional church did, of course, enter the debate with even more determination this time than it did in 1986.

Not only were its biggest guns — the Pope and Mother Teresa — trained on the electorate, but the threat of hellfire and damnation was made all but explicit in Bishop Thomas Flynn's warning that divorced people would not be entitled to the sacraments. Liberals would like to believe, if the referendum is lost, that they were defeated by these traditional antagonists.

But all the evidence is to the contrary. Both William Binchy and Des Hanafin of the Anti-Divorce Camapign were embarrassed by Bishop Flynn's intervention. A parish priest in Bruff who instructed primary school pupils to distribute the bishops' pastoral letter on divorce was unanimously condemned by parents and forced to apologise. And only 7 per cent of voters polled by the MRBI for *The Irish Times* stated that they would vote No primarily on religious grounds. What all of this suggests is that church intervention was at best minimally helpful to the anti-divorce side, at worst counter-productive.

Arguably, indeed, the loss of authority over Irish society by the bishops was a bigger factor in the campaign than their attempts to exercise authority. While many liberals expected the exposure of the bishops in the spate of child abuse scandals to make people more likely to embrace change, it seems in fact to have had the opposite effect.

It needs to be remembered that most Irish Catholics experience the disgrace of their bishops and the loss of trust in their priests not as a liberation but as a trauma. The one thing that seemed stable and trustworthy throughout the breathless decades of change, has suddenly become itself full of dark secrets, of terrible unpredictability, and of dreadful ambiguities. Not only are bishops fleeing the country and priests suddenly disappearing from parishes, but the stories that are emerging cast a shadow on the recent past as well as on the present. They are often stories about what happened in the 1960s and the 1970s, and they throw a sickly retrospective light back on what seemed to be a more orderly time. Not just the present but also the past, seems suddenly darkened.

The effect is that sincere Catholics are, as Bishop Willie Walsh wrote in *The Irish Times* recently, "hurt, sad, angered, frustrated, fearful and insecure". The anger, sparked by the paedophile scandals, may be directed largely at the bishops themselves, but fear and insecurity seldom have the effect of encouraging people to embrace change. The very strong backlash against divorce has shown that many people in Ireland do not share the confidence and optimism about the future that has become almost an orthodoxy in politics and the media.

Some social research has already suggested that this might be so. In a Landsdowne/ Henley Centre study last year, two-thirds of Irish adults said that there will be more fear in Irish society by the year 2000. Half expected less tolerance, less generosity and a less caring society. Much of this fear can be traced to economic failures: 56 per cent expect higher unemployment, and 71 per cent expect crime and violence to be worse. But the divorce debate suggests that it has even wider dimensions. Fear of social breakdown, fear of losing everything that makes Ireland in any way different from other western societies, fear, above all, that the relationships between people will dissolve if they are not enforced by law — these were the raw nerves that the anti-divorce campaign managed to touch.

Politics has been unable to turn such fears into hopes. For the other thing that the divorce debate has told us in no uncertain terms is that political authority has crumbled even more decisively than has the authority of the church. The seven largest political parties in the State — Fianna Fail, Fine Gael, Labour, the Progressive Democrats, Democratic Left, the Green Party and Sinn Fein — all urged a Yes vote. Liberals, paradoxically, believed that the party faithful would do as they were told, and that Fianna

Fail in particular would be able to carry at least the bulk of its supporters with it.

The evidence of every recent by-election, and the bewildering shift in political alliances since the last general election, made that an unlikely proposition. And so it has proved to be. And if that is worrying for political leaders, what should be even more so is that the issue that all of them believe to be of the greatest moment — peace in Northern Ireland — had no discernible influence on the debate. The idea that the peace process has profound implications for the way the Republic conducts itself does not seem to have taken hold. The fundamental belief that political change can make things better seems largely absent at the moment.

With politics in flux and the church in crisis, the family seems to many people to be the only institution that can offer a refuge from uncertainty. When everything else appears temporary and contingent, there seems to be a deep desire to pretend that family life is insulated against the winds of change. It is because the old order is falling apart that the image of people sticking together, come what may, has such a powerful allure. The temptation to retreat from a confusing and uncertain public realm into a warm image of private family bliss seems, for many Irish people, to be irresistible just now.

Whatever the result of the referendum, therefore, it would be a mistake to see it as a decisive turning point. It will be neither a turning back towards a confident assertion of a conservative and secure Catholic identity, nor a confident step into a new era. The debate has revealed conservatives to be extraordinarily pessimistic about the future, seeing Irish society as so fragile that it could be destroyed by changing a single clause in the constitution. And it has shown modernisers that their own optimism is contradicted by the existence of a deeply divided and anxiety-riven society around them.

A narrow victory for either side today will leave Irish society in a condition of rather sour stalemate. If the No side wins by a small margin, it will have to reflect that it has seen its dominance very sharply reduced in just nine years, and that it has merely postponed an inevitable change. Moral crusades need to be won by a convincing margin, not to squeak through by a few votes, leaving nearly half the electorate embittered and increasingly alienated from the church. Equally, if the Yes side wins narrowly, it will do so in the sobering knowledge that nearly half the electorate doesn't share its basic belief that Irish society is getting better. Two cheers may be as much as anyone can manage.

(The electorate voted, by a tiny margin, in favour of the introduction of divorce.)

Making A Drama Of
A Crisis

(This piece was written in November 1994, at the end of the week in which Albert Reynolds lost office as Taoiseach.)

As the political crisis took turn after turn, the language of drama became impossible to avoid. Gay Mitchell told RTE that "there is plenty of material in this performance for a Gilbert and Sullivan operetta." Mary Harney adapted *Hamlet* to tell the Dail that "There's something rotten in the state of Ireland." John Bruton called Albert Reynolds's apparent hesitation about resigning as Fianna Fail leader "a tragedy that has become a farce". Charlie Bird announced that "the plot has taken another twist". Brian Cowen praised his leader for "a class performance". Whether it was operetta or tragedy, farce or whodunnit, everybody agreed that it had all become some kind of show. Irish politics had finally succeeded in making a drama out of a crisis.

The gripping nature of the week's events owes everything to the fact that they were played out before our eyes. Unlike, for instance, the beef tribunal, this scandal acquired the shape of a full-blown drama, with an eager audience, an overwhelming sense of suspense, a stunning denouement and more twist in the tail than Chubby Checker on speed. Through it, Irish public life arrived definitively in the television age. Quite simply, without the televising of the Dail, Albert Reynolds would almost certainly still be Taoiseach, and Mr Justice Harry Whelehan would be looking forward to 20 years as president of the High Court.

Slowly but inexorably, Irish politics has been moving throughout the 1990s from the backrooms to the television screens. The great moments of crisis that people remember from the events that led up to the replacement of Charles Haughey by Albert Reynolds happened on television. When those events are recalled, people will remember Brian Lenihan's ghastly "mature recollection and reflection" interview on the *Six-One News* with Sean Duignan. They will remember Gerry Collins looking into the camera on the same programme and appealing to Albert Reynolds not to "burst up the party". And they will remember Sean Doherty interviewed by Shay Healy for *Nighthawks* in Hell's Kitchen pub in Castlerea, and dropping his hint that "people knew what I was doing" when he tapped the phones of two journalists, thus precipitating the final departure of Charles Haughey.

This week's events, though, are different. The Lenihan, Collins and Doherty outbursts were dramatic reflections on television of political events that were happening off-camera. This week, television was not just reflecting events but driving them. It was the fact that everything was happening live on screen and that it therefore became a drama rather than a story that made it impossible for Albert Reynolds to survive.

Appropriately, the story began on television, with Chris Moore's brilliant hour-long investigative documentary on Father Brendan Smyth for Ulster Television's *Counterpoint*. It is striking that the image at the back of people's minds this week was not a news photograph or even a piece of news footage, but a stylised, slow-motion black-and-white sequence of Brendan Smyth in clerical garb walking towards the camera and into a schoolyard. That image from the Counterpoint documentary, played over and over again in the last 10 days became central to the crisis — a tangible and memorable image of evil which gave a clear moral centre to complicated and otherwise obscure events in Cabinet room and the Attorney General's office.

Unlike the other television programme which could have ended Albert Reynolds's career, the 1991 *World In Action* investigation of the links between Goodman International and Fianna Fail, though, this story stayed on screen. The beef scandal vanished off our screens and into a room in Dublin Castle where the cameras were not allowed to go. Its images on television became the flickering processions of men in dark suits with bulging briefcases crossing the castle courtyard behind a news reporter trying to explain in three minutes what had happened inside. The real courtroom drama of events indoors never happened for the viewing public. It remained a second-hand story rather than a first-hand drama.

I remember watching the three extraordinary days of Albert Reynolds's sworn evidence and thinking that if only it were happening live on television, he would probably have had to resign as Taoiseach then. But hidden from the camera's baleful eye, he survived, and the public gradually lost patience with a story that seemed too long, too obscure and too abstract.

The same thing could well have happened with the political ramifications of Harry Whelehan's appointment to the High Court presidency. Many of the original issues surrounding Labour's opposition to that appointment arose directly from the beef tribunal. And like the tribunal itself they remained, for most of the public, abstract and therefore seemingly unimportant. For all the huffing and puffing, it is clear that if things had stayed at that level, Labour would have lumped the appointment even if they didn't like it.

Even when the Brendan Smyth affair began to intrude on the argument, the precise details could still have remained abstruse. The processing, or rather non-processing, of extradition warrants, and the internal affairs of the Attorney General's office are not the stuff of national crisis, however vital the stories that lie behind them. Only because the Brendan Smyth affair came with built-in television images did a serious issue of public policy become a national crisis.

It is unlikely that, when they agreed to let cameras into the Dail, politicians thought that *Oireachtas Report* would ever become the most rivetting programme on television. Yet the very things that make the Dail normally so dull to watch — the formality, the set-pieces, the ritualised antagonisms — made the events on Wednesday into brilliant television. Television is at its best when the stuff of reality is slightly stylised, retaining the appearance of real life without its messiness. Wednesday's drama was precisely that — a real drama unfolding within the arena of a formalised debate, with its own rules and conventions.

Having watched Tuesday's events from the Dail press gallery and Wednesday's on television, I was struck by how much clearer and more dramatic everything seemed on the screen than in the flesh. Television filtered out the distractions — the rows of empty seats, the whispered conversations, the fidgeting TDs, the random and ritual heckling — and made the conflicts clearer. It also allowed for a running commentary on the events that were part of the drama, the TDs and party leaders emerging onto the forecourt of Leinster House to express their ever-increasing incredulity, the impact of the crisis washing up on the serene shores of the bishops' meeting in Maynooth, the poignant glimpse of Albert Reynolds in his car on the *Six-One News*, telling us that "I'm never disappointed with life. I take life as it comes."

Even the early chaos of Wednesday morning was rivetting. Pat Rabbitte filled the void with wild imaginings when he stood up to ask about a document that would rock the foundations of the State. Albert Reynolds seemed to add substance to the notion that something extraordinary was unfolding when he spoke of "a very serious matter" and promised the "full, full, full facts". Cardinal Daly appeared from Maynooth to scotch "absurd" rumours.

When *Oireachtas Report* started at four o'clock and John O'Donoghue asked the question on everyone's mind — "What is going to happen next?" — it was no mere teaser. Over the course of the afternoon, Ireland had entered an imaginative hyperspace in which anything seemed possible and everything, however bizarre, seemed credible. The earth's crust, in the words of Georg Buchner, seemed suddenly thin.

The opening shots came close to suggesting anarchy. There was no Ceann Comhairle in the chair. Neither the Taoiseach nor the Minister for Justice was to be seen. The Government Chief Whip was moving around the opposition benches, muttering into the ears of the other leaders. The Taoiseach arrived and added to the anarchy by telling the Dail that he could discover nothing about "a certain letter". Someone from the Attorney General's office was arriving in Frankfurt at 6.25. Someone else was lost on the west coast of America, California dreaming while the State twisted in the wind. Mary Harney asked why Maire Geoghegan Quinn was absent. Albert Reynolds insisted that "I am not in the business of hiding anything or covering up." But what was supposed to be under the non-existent cover? What was the colour of the dog that wasn't barking?

We were left dangling over the precipice. And in such a state, any revelation, anything that would give substance to the products of our imaginations, would have extraordinary force. In ordinary circumstances, the news that the Taoiseach had failed to mention an obscure extradition case in a speech to the Dail would fall into the category of noises off. But because the stage was set for its entrance in a great and epic drama, it carried the force of revelation. The mortified look on the face of Bertie Ahern, sitting beside his leader, gave visual immediacy to an admission whose actual substance was hard to fathom.

And there was more. While John Bruton, Mary Harney and Prionsias de Rossa were putting shape on the confusion, another leading player was waiting in the wings with stunning new revelations. Dick Spring seemed to relish the role. He teased his audience by starting off with studied nonchalance, cracking jokes and smiling. Then he turned up the suspense by hinting at what he was going to say without revealing what it was: "I must outline the events of the last few hours". By the time he unveiled his revelation that the Taoiseach knew about the new information before his speech on Tuesday, the reaction was audible, indeed, almost tangible. A long *oooh* of exhalation rumbled beneath a high-pitched whistle of awe. The drama had reached the climax towards which it had moving with inexorable force.

Even some of those in the chamber, though, did not understand that a drama of this kind must end with a stage full of corpses. Brian Cowen still seemed to believe that what had happened belonged to the normal cut-and-thrust of parliamentary conflict, that it had not become a great national drama. When he went on *Prime Time* on Wednesday night with Prionsias de Rossa and Sean Barrett, he was like a character from another play altogether, a sad reprise of the last days of Charles Haughey. Like Gerry Collins and Brian Lenihan rolled into one he staggered from emotional bluster to wounded self-justification.

He could not grasp the obvious fact that the drama had turned the revelation about the new information from the humdrum world of political cliches to the last act of an epic performance. He still thought, as he repeatedly and desperately insisted, that it was "a technical legal point... an oversight... a totally unjustifiable reason not to continue with government." Like the boy on the burning deck, he remained steadfast amidst the flames : "I defend my party and leader at all times". But the ship was going down, and his wiser colleagues were swimming for dear life.

Television had made the crisis public property and taken it well beyond the reach of such desperate defences. While we have become used to the idea that television has debased politics, this time it gave real substance to politics. There could be no closed circuits and no private arrangements. Just this once, we caught history on the hop and knew that we were on the same level as our rulers. We saw what they saw, shared their confusions, learned things as they learned them, gasped when they gasped, and drew the same, inevitable, conclusions. Just this once, television allowed to us to be players in the drama.

Permission To Speak

(This piece was written in June 1996.)

There seems to be a general consensus that there is too much talk on RTE and that Gay Byrne has had his day. Both of these perceptions may be accurate enough in themselves, but something tells me that there is, behind them, a deeper disgruntlement. Both Gay Byrne and RTE have played critical roles in the opening up of discussion in Ireland. They have, over four decades, redefined what it is permissible to talk about. And I get the feeling that, for many people, that process has gone far enough. A lot of what we have had to talk about has been very unpleasant indeed, and we are tired of listening to it. We wonder if it would not be better if, after all, the worms were to crawl quietly back under the stones. A court report I read last month made me think again about this.

In September, 1993, I went on the *Late Late Show*. I had been writing here about the Stay Safe programme in schools and the campaign against it by right-wing Catholic groups. The programme is aimed at giving children a language in which they can discuss bullying and abuse, and an idea of how to report it. It is now being used successfully in virtually every primary school in the Republic, but at the time there was a very strong and well-organised campaign to oppose it. Some of the opponents subsequently came to greater public prominence in the No Divorce campaign. Others are Catholic priests, concerned, as one of them put it, that 'the claim that a child owns its own body is at odds with Christian tradition.'

When I was asked to debate the issue on the *Late Late*, I wasn't sure how to respond. I know enough about television to know how crude it can be, how inadequately it deals with complex and sensitive questions, how it can not merely obscure the truth but actively distort it. I was worried about whether such a debate might merely serve to give a platform for the views of obscurantist cranks. I had also, to be honest, grown weary of a subject on which I had said a lot to little effect and thought I had nothing else to say.

I decided, however, to do the show, largely because some of the black propaganda used against the Stay Safe programme had been so vile — claiming, for instance, that it was called the 'Safe Sex' programme, and that it 'prepared children for abuse' — that there was a real danger that some parents might have been genuinely frightened by it. But this consideration only just outweighed the misgivings.

After the show, I was still very unsure about whether I had made the right decision. The debate was a typical televisual set-piece, more concerned with the drama of absolute oppositions than with establishing truths or imparting information. After it, there was a feeling of utter pointlessness. Here was an issue which, to me at least, could not be more clear-cut: whether or not schools should help children to protect themselves from bullying and abuse by talking to adults they could trust.

The discussion seemed, from the inside, merely to have taken that moral clarity and disguised it as yet another round in an endless cultural war between tradition and change in Ireland. That impression was subsequently strengthened by the fact that the campaign against Stay Safe melted away when the divorce referendum appeared on the horizon and the right-wing Catholics moved on to what were, for them, bigger targets.

What I didn't know was that in a housing estate somewhere in County Offaly, an 11 year-old boy was watching the *Late Late Show* that night with his mother and a neighbour, a man of 75, who usually watched it with them. When the item about the Stay Safe programme came on, the neighbour had become uncomfortable. After a few minutes, he made an excuse and left.

The mother could feel a sense of expectation. Her son then asked her what sexual abuse was. When she told him, he asked her how she would react if one of her children had been abused. She said she would be supportive. The boy said "Mammy, I was abused." He then told his mother that the neighbour who had been watching the *Late Late* with them a few minutes earlier had raped him about twenty times in the previous four years.

The boy had stayed in the neighbour's house to help look after him when he was ill. The man had sometimes plied the boy with vodka or whiskey until he fell asleep and then assaulted him. According to the boy, he also "told him daft things about men and religion and he told him men could have babies."

The mother contacted a solicitor shortly afterwards, and she and her son were put in touch with the Midland Health Board. Last September, a complaint was made to the Garda, and last month the neighbour, having pleaded guilty to two sample charges of rape and two of sexual assault, was jailed for five years.

This story is, amongst other things, a tribute to Gay Byrne, whose broadcasting career is now apparently entering its home stretch. It is very hard to think of any other circumstances or any other place in which a 78 year-old man, an 11 year-old boy and a middle-aged woman would all be sitting down at ten o'clock on a Friday night watching a debate about the prevention of child abuse between an obscure journalist and a barely less obscure academic. And it is very hard to imagine that, after the *Late Late* is gone, any television programme will ever again have the kind of routine place in people's lives that allows for such a direct link between reality and the stylised drama of the small screen.

But the story is also a necessary reminder that there is still, in Ireland, a great deal to be said. Those of us who work in the media become affected by a paradoxical mixture of weary futility and self-centred arrogance in which we both undervalue and over-rate the work we do. We get tired of dealing with the same issues time and again, and often lose the conviction that there is any point in saying them. But we also assume that because we are weary of an issue, its importance has somehow diminished. We forget why it arose in the first place — because it touches the lives of the people we are supposed to serve.

Talking about things does, sometimes, change them just as refusing to talk about them allows them to happen. The man convicted of rape in Offaly also admitted to gardai that he had abused his grand-nephew years earlier. He got away with it. That young man went to England where he subsequently suffered a nervous breakdown that halted a promising career. Fifteen years ago, what had been done to him was not a subject for public discussion in the newspapers or on television, and because it wasn't, we thought the place was much nicer than it really was. But if it had been, the abuser might not have been free to move on to another victim and destroy another life. It may be more pleasant to fill the silence with happy music, but there are very good reasons why the tongue set free by radio and television should never be tied again.